IT ALL GOES TOGETHER

IT ALL GOES TOGETHER

Selected Essays by

ERIC GILL

NEW YORK : THE DEVIN-ADAIR COMPANY : MCMXLIV

This book has been produced under wartime conditions. As in the case of Gill's Autobiography, the typography has been designed to conform with the principles of functional simplicity that Eric Gill preached. We should like to have used his Perpetua type, examples of which are shown among the illustrations, but none is yet available in America, so Baskerville was again selected as being somewhat akin in crisp clarity to Perpetua.

Since Eric Gill's work is so widely distributed among private collectors, the illustrations were made from reproductions rather than from originals. While it is obviously next to impossible to achieve by machine processes the exact effects of printing from wood blocks, the greatest possible care was taken to prevent loss of value and detail.

The publishers wish to acknowledge their indebtedness to the following: The Weyhe Galleries for making available most of the illustrations used; Graham Carey for the reproduction of his carved bedstead; David Hennessy for the autographed snapshot of Gill which appears on the jacket; and Lewis F. White for the time and interest he took in seeing the book through its various stages.

INTRODUCTION

I KNEW Eric Gill in England as a lovable person and as an artist, and after 1917 never saw him again. We were both of us beginning to grow up then; and since then we have corresponded regularly and were in very close agreement about fundamentals; and so it would not be untrue to say that we went to school together and grew up together, although apart. This association and coopera- tion must be my excuse for an Introduction to a collection of his essays that really needs no advertisement.

In Mrs. Gill's brief *Preface* she mentions Eric's conception of the "priesthood of craftsmanship" and his great fight for human "freedom to do that work for which a man's nature best fits him." He said himself that he invented a religion and found that it was Roman Christianity: he might also have said that he reinvented a human way of working, and found that it was that of all tradi- tional societies and Plato's way. For it is just in those societies, in which all contingent problems are really approached in the light of first principles, that, as A. M. Hocart said, *"chaque occupation est un sacerdoce . . . les métiers et les rites ne peuvent se dis- tinguer exactement";* and Plato defined justice as the liberty "to go about the business that is properly one's own by nature." This amounts to saying that Eric's was not a personal point of view, but simply a true one, that he had made his own. He was not "think- ing for himself," but assenting to credible propositions; and he was, accordingly, a man of faith.

On the one hand, a free man with a vocation and responsibil- ity; on the other, industrial man, "economically determined," and irresponsible. On the one hand, production for use; on the other,

v

for profit. On the one hand a making by art (it is not without reason that we call the manufactures of the Stone Age "artifacts") and
every man a special kind of artist; on the other an industry without art (Ruskin's "brutality"), unredeemed by the existence of a
class of privileged "artists" whose work need have no use, and if it
is "applied" is then no longer "fine." Eric was never tired of pointing out these symptoms of our modern schizophrenia. It is no
wonder that he called our modern way of life "neither human nor
normal nor Christian." Others have called it "anomalous and
monstrous" and "a curse to humanity." We had the illusion of
"progress" and have made a desert; we aspired to develop our
individualities at all costs, and have become a herd; we wanted
to be "free," and are more than ever the helpless subjects of our
ruling passions. By "civilised" men, we now do not mean cultured
men, but industrialised men; "civilised" men are those who employ the same mechanical techniques to "master nature"; the rest
are savages, or at any rate "backward peoples." We have in fact
destroyed *their* cultures. We can hardly believe that there still are
peoples who thank God that they are not yet as we are, and who
fear that they may be reduced to our level.

We have proposed a "century of the common man" in terms
of common insects; an age of men so round that they can be fitted
into any hole. For, as Znaniecki [1] says: "It matters not whether
the present-day factory worker is, as regards the duration and in-
tensity of his exertion, in a better or worse condition than the
savage hunter or the artisan of the Middle Ages. The point that
does matter is that his mind has no share in determining the aims
of his work and that his body, as an instrument of independent
creative power, has lost most of its significance. Hence his mind,
divorced from creative activity, turns in the main to the problem
of satisfying the needs of his primitive animal appetites; while his
body having lost, in his own eyes, well-nigh all its importance as
an instrument of skilled production, interests him almost exclu-

---

[1] Quoted in A. J. Krzesinski, *Is Modern Culture Doomed?* 1942, p. 54.

sively as a source of pleasure and discomfort." And as Msgr. G. B. O'Toole adds, "the eclecticist and pragmatic philosophies of education in vogue amongst us have acted like a solvent on American culture, liquidating all the eternal and spiritual values, sparing only the phenomenal husk of civilisation, the upshot being that while still a civilised people, we are no longer a cultured one. . . . . Nor is commercialism culture's only foe; in our machinery, too, it has a formidable enemy. For in mechanised industry all the creative work is confined to the inventor of the machine; the operators become as automatic as the machines they tend." Nor must we suppose that the capitalist and consumer (you and I) for whom all these mechanics labor, can escape: on the contrary, our "innumerable time-saving devices do not afford Americans leisure to culture their persons, but simply enable them to have more irons in the fire. The net result is that we do no creative work, produce nothing calculated to give either ourselves or others genuine artistic pleasure. From this point of view, the standardised products of our mills and factories are a disgrace to American civilisation—trumpery furniture . . . miles of dingy warehouses. And this rubbish heap has been bought at a frightful cost of both human and natural resources. . . . In the space of two centuries we have impoverished our soil and depleted its organic and inorganic resources more than the Chinese have theirs in the course of four millenniums." [1] It is also a part of the price of the rubbish heap that the Western nations hate and distrust one another, and are collectively feared or hated by all African and Asiatic peoples. How could it have been otherwise? For what does "Free Enterprise" mean? It means "his hand against every man, and every man's hand against him."

"Impoverished the soil" is a phrase of cultural as well as agricultural significance. For all these things have not happened by chance, but by a diabolical, although often unconscious—subconscious—intention; they are the outcome of a desperate effort to

---

[1] From the *Foreword* to Krzesinski, *loc. cit.*

live by "bread alone" factory made, and preferably pre-sliced.

In making up our minds that "such knowledge as is not empirical is meaningless," [1] we resigned ourselves to a meaningless world of "impoverished reality," a ground in which there could no longer grow "those foods by which the wings of the soul are nourished and grow,—wisdom, goodness and all such qualities." "Qualities," or "values": ay, there's the rub. For these are "colorless, shapeless and intangible," and though we are still able to give a positive content to negative terms (such as "independence"), we have lost the habit of indication by exclusion *(via remotionis)* and it is difficult for us to think of intangibles as "the essential realities that are the proper object of all true knowledge." [2] Now it is quite true that the founders of modern materialism "did not deny the existence of spiritual or ideal entities; in fact, they asserted their existence. But they did neglect these entities; they very largely confined their systematic expositions to an explanation of the whole of nature in terms of an impoverished reality. . . . Under these conditions, it is quite understandable that this concept of nature soon became so familiar that complete faith attached to it, and it was accepted as self-evident truth. It is equally understandable that this concept should undermine belief and faith in any other realms or aspects of reality. For these other types of being could not be reduced to the attribute of extension," [3]—they could not be measured or weighed.

Eric Gill was very much alive, and so could never have been contented with an art for art's sake or knowledge for its own sake, as the child is contented who likes to hear a watch tick and then wants to see what makes the wheels go round. Watches, for Eric, were not toys, but timepieces.

The simplicity of greatness enabled him to penetrate the falla-

---

[1] A. B. Keith, *Aitareya Aranyaka*, p. 42. This almost classical confession of materialism is the more remarkable in that these are not the words of a scientist, but of a great orientalist and an accomplished scholar of the humanities.

[2] *Phaedrus* 246 E—247 E.

[3] I. Jenkins, in the *Journal of Philosophy*, 39, 1942, p. 543.

cies of modern "knowledge," and to see clearly that, as Plato says, "the possession of the sciences as a whole, if it does not include the best, will in some few cases aid but more often harm the owner." [1] He saw this with particular clarity in the fields of psychology and sociology. He realised that modern psychology sets up again a concept of Fate, not as this concept was traditionally understood, but in the "fatalistic" sense that involves the denial of human responsibility and abolishes "sin"; human failings being no longer thought of as faults, but as misfortunes, the working of a malign "fate." "When," as he says, "the psychologist says 'it is heredity, it is early environment, it is a complex,' we applaud. . . . We have erected, as is natural, a system of industry exactly corresponding to our philosophy and depending upon it. *Actus sequitur esse*. We do not believe men are responsible; we have made them irresponsible . . . in the world in which the man of money is king the workman is nothing but a tool. It is common knowledge: the workman is only a tooth on a wheel. What he makes with his hands is not his responsibility and its only concern to his master is its saleability. And as these irresponsible tools are the great majority of the population, they provide the biggest market . . . and in the end it has necessarily come about that the only things which it is possible to sell are those which no intelligent person finds it possible to buy. . . . There is no remedy but that which man alone has the power to apply. . . . He must reaffirm the freedom of his will and his consequent responsibility for all his deeds and works. . . . The factory system is unchristian primarily because it deprives workmen of responsibility for their work."

Eric had no illusions about the virtues of the common man. "Trade unionism," he says, "does what it can to make labour more expensive, but it makes no bones about servility. . . . Your trade-union leader is your typical rationalist . . . he gets his philosophy ready-made from the very people he is fighting." Who ever heard

---

[1] II *Alcibiades,* 144 D.

of a trade-unionist striking for the right to make goods of a better quality? So one of the defects of the factory system is precisely that "it prevents Trades Unions from becoming Trades Guilds." It has often been said that "a man can be a very good Catholic in a factory." So can a man be a very good, and even a supremely good, Christian in the arena or under torture.

As Schweitzer, too, says: "From every side and in the most varied ways it is dinned into him—the man of to-day—that the truths and convictions which he needs for life must be taken by him from the associations *that have rights over him*. . . . The seed of scepticism has germinated. In fact, the modern man has no longer any spiritual self-confidence at all." [1] "To disbelieve is the natural way of the mob"; [2] and our ways of thought and our "education" have forbidden to their victims the aristocratic privilege of an affirmative belief.

No one has ever better understood than Eric Gill, who was anything but a lazy man, the fallacy of the modern conception of leisure and the modern Utopia of the "leisure state"; for this is not a leisure at all in the classical sense of a *working with ease* but only an idleness and what Plato calls a "living in sports always." At no other time in the history of the world has the apolaustic life been set up as the ideal term of an otherwise indefinite "progress," but whether we like it or not, "the thing to which our present confusion is leading is the thing called *the Leisure State*. . . . All necessary work being done by machinery . . . the human race will be freed from 'the curse of Adam' and will be free to contemplate the 'eternal verities' in the long leisure thus secured . . . and contemplation will vary from the pure 'art' of the abstractionists and surrealists to the pure enjoyment of young men and women protected by reliable contraceptives."

Why does the chain-belt operator, like a chain-gang prisoner

---

[1] A. Schweitzer, *My Life and Thought*, 1935 ed., pp. 256, 257.
[2] Anonymous gloss on *Phaedo* 69 E.

counting days until his time expires, watch the clock impatiently? Because when he is at work he is doing what he likes least, and in this matter of wanting the day to be over shows that he is still human after all; human, because it is *in*human to have to work unintelligently and irresponsibly for one's living; human, because anyone who has to support his family by work he detests *ought* to be discontented. I have seen workmen—carpenters and painters, in a "backward" society—who neither watched a clock nor "punched" it: men who were not paid extra for overtime, but who *insisted* on working overtime (by candlelight), to their own pecuniary loss (this was not piecework) because they loved their work so much that they could not bear to lay down their tools. A "manufacturer's" paradise? not at all, for these men could easily have been taught to make their labour more expensive, but as it was they were not working for a master, but directly for a consumer; *they* were the manu-facturer himself. Moreover, under these conditions, which are essentially those of all "backward" societies, the needs of the soul and body are satisfied together, and there is no class distinction of "artists" from "craftsmen." It is to these "savage" levels of culture that "civilisation" must revert, if men are not to revolt against it. For on what are revolutions based but injustice (denial of opportunity to do the work for which one is fitted by nature) and discontent (engendered by distasteful employment)?

Within the limits of an Introduction it would be impossible to do full justice to Eric's many-sidedness. Of his powers as an artist I shall not say anything here except to remark that the precision of his writing corresponds to that of the lettering of which he was an acknowledged master. I shall only allude to one of his outstanding qualities: an ability to recognise the truth, not only in Christian contexts, but wherever he found it. One might not have expected this in a convert, and indeed it is a comparatively rare quality even in those who are born to the faith and have examples in St. Thomas Aquinas or even in Calvin that might be followed in this respect. As Walter Shewring says, Eric "accepted every consequence of the Ambrosian principle embraced by St. Thomas Aquinas, that *all* truth is from the Holy Ghost." [1] It was this open mind, and neither a "tolerance" nor a latitudinarian point of view, that enabled him to write of Indian religion and art without in any way compromising his own explicit and devoted adherence to the forms of Roman Christianity. He told me once that he had realised that the doctrines of Hinduism and those of Christianity were essentially the same.

The most essential quality of life is its sense of purpose; all things seek their ultimate perfection. President Roosevelt has said that "we cannot be content, no matter how high the general standard of living may be, if some fraction of our people—whether it be one-third or one-fifth or one-tenth—is ill-fed, ill-clothed, ill-housed and insecure." Only the words "ill-clothed" assure us that he is referring, not to animals in a zoo, but to human beings. Between this rather limited conception of well-being and the dictum of Stuart Chase that "a modern economic system must maintain a relatively high speed or crack up . . . National frugality means . . . unemployment" there is a sinister connection. For, as Boethius says, *avaritiae nihil satis est.*

A material standard of living to be for ever "improved" can have no bearing on *contentment,* i.e., freedom from want (-ing). Civilisation has even been described in terms of a perpetual creation of new "wants"; which are no sooner satisfied, than they become "necessities." In this way, as Leopold Ziegler, amongst others, so clearly realises, we are "driven about by a material hunger, which in accordance with the will of finance must never be appeasable," and all men, even the rich, are "doomed to a poverty hitherto undreamed of." "From this point of view," as he continues, "modern finance reveals itself as the enemy of society, yes, even as the destroyer of society, inasmuch as it crudely transgresses moral and religious messages of the higher order." What

---

[1] *Blackfriars* (Eric Gill Memorial Number), February, 1941, p. 88.

was lately said by the Pasha of Marrakesh, that "We do not want the incredible American way of life. We want the world of the Koran," was stated as forcibly by Eric Gill, by his way of life, which was in accordance with the command to "Seek first the kingdom of God and *His* justice, and all these things shall be added to you." *Intellige ut credas:* when we realise that *dikaio-sune,* the word for "justice" here, is the same that Plato defines in the vocational terms of a freedom to pursue the callings to which we are severally and variously summoned by our own innate qualities, then it becomes apparent that the scriptural promise is one that *must* be fulfilled, *if* we accept its premises,— and so, as Plato adds, that "more will be done, and better, and more easily than in any other way."

Latin *facere* (in manu-*facture*), like Sanskrit *kar* (in *karma,* work), to make, had once no other meaning than to "sacri-fice," that is, "make holy"; and there is no necessary distinction of sacred from profane tasks, or of a fine from an applied art. *Laborare est orare* is hardly a text that could be hung in a modern factory. Work *is* prayer: yes, but only when our work is voluntary, not when it is economically determined. There is no true prayer under compulsion; he prayeth best who loveth best,—all things, but most of all *his own work.*

A great modern exponent of the Philosophia Perennis has re-marked: "The West was Christian in the Middle Ages; it is so no longer. Should anyone say that it may yet become so again, then no one is more anxious than I that this should be so, and that it should happen earlier than we might expect from what we see around us. But let there be no mistake about it; when it happens, the day of the modern world will be over—*le monde moderne aura vécu.*" [1] The modern world *will* come to an end. But it would be optimistic to imagine that we are looking on at its finish now: industrialism and other products of the free-for-all philosophy, which we call in India the "law of the sharks," have still in

---

[1] René Guénon, *La crise du monde moderne,* 1927, p. 201.

the making for us bigger and better wars to come. However this may be, the least that can be said of Eric Gill's whole life and work, or to express it better, whole life-work, is that it has helped to prepare the way for the end of our world and the coming of a more reasonable, happier and better one. And that is also why, if not already prepared by temperament and training to agree, you who read his essays will be enraged by his seriousness and his logic, and will call him an impractical idealist, one of those dreamers who insist on talking about "what ought to be" instead of allowing "progress" itself to take care of "what will be," —you whose more "practical" ideal is represented by the *status quo ante bellum,*—to be ameliorated only by the civilian benefits to be derived from the application of war-time inventions to domestic convenience, as soon as the manufacturer is released from the immediate necessity of providing the instruments of death, and is free to provide us with the prefabricated houses in which we shall be allowed to live through the next brief period of internecine "peace."

A writer in *Common Sense,* August 1943, remarks in this connection: "Whether the results be socially or esthetically desirable is another question, but at least we are abandoning nineteenth century handicraft methods for more efficient and sensible modes of production." It is, perhaps, the peculiarity of an era of production for profit, rather than "for good use," that methods leading to results of which the desirability is "another question" can be described as "efficient and sensible"!

ANANDA K. COOMARASWAMY.

Museum of Fine Arts,
Boston.

CONTENTS

Introduction, by Ananda K. Coomaraswamy v

Preface, by Mary Gill xvii

1. Idiocy or Ill-Will (1922) 3
2. The Lord's Song (1934) 14
3. The Factory System and Christianity (1918) 21
4. David Jones (1930) 28
5. Clothing without Cloth (1931) 34
6. John Ruskin (1934) 45
7. All Art Is Propaganda (1935) 48
8. It All Goes Together (1936) 51
9. Eating Your Cake (1936) 57
10. Sculpture on Machine-Made Buildings (1936) 61
11. Art in England Now (1937) 88
12. Art and Business (1940) 96
13. The Human Person and Society (1940) 99
14. Art (1940) 113
15. Work (1940) 122
16. Private Property (1940) 128
17. Education for What? (1940) 135
18. Peace and Poverty (1939) 142
19. Art and Education (1940) 148
20. Five Hundred Years of Printing (1940) 152
21. The Leisure State (1940) 157
22. Secular and Sacred in Modern Industry (1940) 163
23. And Who Wants Peace? (1936) 179

A list of books by Eric Gill 189

Illustrations 193

Leave to reprint these writings has freely been granted by all concerned. Thanks are accordingly expressed: For Nos. 1 and 3, to Mr. Hilary Pepler; for Nos. 2 and 5, to the Golden Cockerel Press; for No. 4, to *Artwork;* for No. 6, to the Ruskin Society and the Cambridge University Press; for No. 7, to Messrs. Lawrence and Wishart; for No. 8, to *The Cross and the Plough;* for No. 9, to *The Penrose Annual;* for No. 10, to the City of Birmingham School of Printing; for No. 12, to Messrs. P. E. Gane; for No. 13, to the Peace Pledge Union; for No. 14, to *Blackfriars;* for Nos. 15 and 16, to the *Catholic Herald;* for No. 17, to *The Schoolmaster;* for No. 19, to *Athene;* for No. 21 to *The Clergy Review.*

PREFACE

In publishing these essays of my husband, it is my wish to send them as a message from him to the workmen craftsmen of England and America and the world—men whom he loved and whose welfare he had so much at heart—the 'Priesthood of craftsmanship', to use his own words. His message was prophetic: he saw to what state of things, to what kind of world Industrialism was leading us; and all that he wished to say he said clearly, returning again and again to those primary truths which experience showed him to need repeating most.

I hope that those who read this book will more fully understand in what sense and in what spirit my husband desired the workman's freedom—freedom to work responsibly, freedom to do that work for which a man's nature best fits him—and with what rightness and power he defended the fundamentals on which all making rests.

MARY GILL.

Pigotts, Hughenden,
England.

IT ALL GOES TOGETHER

CHAPTER I

IDIOCY OR ILL-WILL

I

WE WERE staying at G——. I must tell you the sort of place it is. First of all, it is on a little mountain of its own, and it is a very little town. There is one street of about thirty houses on each side with a castle and a church and a nunnery at one end and a gateway at the other. It is all built of stone, and nothing has been built since the seventeenth century simply because there is no room for more. There are much higher mountains all round, the air is noisy with the bells of the cows.

You know the Swiss are marvellously tidy people. So the whole thing is beautifully in order, and not ruinously picturesque. Moreover the whole population—and there are several hundred children—is Catholic, except an American artist and his wife, who are said to be, like the Jew in Aberdeen, too poor to leave, and we were told that the postman is a Socialist and a sower of discord. The church is a good plain building, and the *curé*, a real shepherd, has a *vicaire* as holy and as hard-working as himself. Many of the men of the place are herdsmen and cheesemakers on the mountains, and some are foresters. The women are—mothers. I said there were hundreds of children. There is a washing-place in the middle of the street, a fountain at which they take turns. There is always washing going on and always the sound of water. You see the place; it is what is called primitive, it may also be

3

called highly civilized, and, in any case, it is what the Catholic Church has made it.

But though it is not a ruin, it has its Catholicism, perhaps, too much as a *physical* habit and this is the devil's opportunity. He is not neglectful of it. There are beginnings of corruption. There are chocolate factories within a few miles—and a milk factory is nearer still. There are tourists within its walls. The local handicrafts are dying out. The people are seduced by the shops of the big town. They make less and buy more. The things in their own little shop are mostly the cheap nasty product of the outside industrialism. The young women wear the rotten clothes of—suburban Paris. Their crockery comes from Stoke-on-Trent, perhaps. Probably the rising tide cannot be turned back. Meanwhile it remains a holy place, a fertile island not yet submerged, a place of pilgrimage.

Well, we were staying at the hotel. . . . It is a very nice hotel. In the *salle à manger* you sit at a long table, and as we cannot speak any French, and no one (except one very nice serving maid) spoke English, we were enjoying real peace.

Then they arrived.

They were three. Middle class, middle age, middle wit, and seeing that they were neither men nor mothers, one might call them middle sex, though at least one of them came from Manchester. They were really quite nice. Two were silent, and one was deaf, slightly but unmistakably. Our peace was at an end for she insisted on talking. They really *were* quite nice. They called one another "dear," at least she did. She sat opposite to me; the other two sat several places away on my right. I never heard what they said. I think they spoke with difficulty.

They were having a holiday, and were by way of being botanists. She asked me if I liked flowers, and when I said, "Oh, yes," she thought I meant "not much." Of course she knew we were English because we talked their language among ourselves, but that would have made no difference, for she talked English boldly to everyone as one who went about doing good. She was very good-

4

natured. She was really quite "dear." It is difficult to blame her.

I knew it was inevitable—besides, the worst that can happen to me is less than I deserve—but she began very badly.

She said: "Isn't it all quaint and old-fashioned?"

I supposed she might be right. She scented disapproval. She said: "I suppose you are very fond of everything that's old."

I said it didn't make any odds to me whether it was old or new, provided it was good.

She said: "But don't you believe in progress?"

"Dear Lord," I thought.

I said: "Progress towards what?"

She said: "Oh, to all that is highest and best."

"Dear Lord," I prayed.

I said: "Well, of course I do. But the point is that in a place like this they've pretty well got there. The only trouble is to stay there. But the devil is creeping in."

She said: "What did you say?" I told you she was deaf.

I said again: *"The devil is creeping in."*

She said: "Oh, I thought you said *error.*"

That was all, and how magnificently enough! The church bells rang, and we went to Mass. It was quaint enough for them to come too. So they did. Afterwards I hit on the solution of their trouble.

Error—the devil. The devil—error. Surely it is much the same thing, and yet this is one of the devil's best moves. This is just exactly where he has got the modern world caught. You see error connotes mistakes and misunderstandings. It suggests the darkness of ignorance, the lapse of intelligence. It is intellect gone wrong; and are we not all intellectual and thus prone to error?

But the devil! He calls up a very different order of things. You don't, somehow, connect the devil with the idea of making mistakes. The devil isn't so much a "wrong un" as a "bad un." The devil is not an idiot; he is a sinner. His is an evil will. See what a difference it makes! You say, "error is creeping in" and it is really quite a comforting thought. A lot of good people are

5

making mistakes. That can soon be put right by the spread of elementary education and a sound system of secondary schools and universities! But say "the devil is creeping in" and either you mean nothing at all, or you mean something very uncomfortable indeed. You mean a lot of good people are turning bad. And how can *that* be put right? It is so much easier to erect asylums for idiots than to persuade sinners to go to confession. That was her trouble. That is everybody's trouble. We prefer to call it error. We refuse to call it ill-will. We turn to a new line of thought. We refuse to return to an old line of conduct. There are the two categories then in human affairs, the intellectual and the moral, as there are the two functions in the human soul, the intellect and the will. And the trouble to-day is that a most remarkable reversal of things has taken place. The intellect is gone on the loose and the will has been chained up!

The movement of thought during the last few centuries has turned our brains. Thought shall be free, we said. And in the process of what we called "free thinking," we came to the conclusion that there could be no such thing as "free will." How the devil laughed! It has been his greatest obstacle, that notion that men could only think what was true, but could do what they chose. He had chosen to hate God, and it was his ambition to persuade men to love themselves. From time to time he had had considerable success. But always he was hindered because of this thing called responsibility. Too many men continued to feel responsible for their actions—too many clung to the notion of a space that was not curved, a truth that was not relative. But now, from his point of view, everything is happily changed. Thought is free—men say they can think what they like. Will is bound—men say that the unceasing and universal "laws" of cause and effect have freed them from sin. Of course *you* can see it is all nonsense. But nevertheless the two million readers of the *Daily Mail* are more enlightened.

The fact is that the phrase "free thought," however useful it may be politically and as a stick to beat Popes with, is bad philosophy: it is a contradiction in terms. Thought is not free and cannot

6

be free. You can *say* two and two make five, but that is doing, not thinking. That is an act of will, not of thought.

"Whatever can be *thought* is true, but what *can* be thought?" Upon the other hand, not everything that can be done is good.

The modern world, denying dogmatic truth and free-will, is pleased to suppose that it can think what it chooses, and to solace itself by saying that sin does not exist and that evil can be removed by Act of Parliament . . . by the regimentation of the poor and their sterilization . . . by compulsory arbitration . . . by insurance.

I wish all this had occurred to me at the table. I didn't see it quickly enough; and afterwards she gave me no opportunity. She had found a man who really did "like flowers," a proper botanist who made a special business of finding rock funguses. He was a Catholic priest. He was wiser than I. He didn't mention the devil.

II

Let us go back then. We have in the modern world, as opposed to the ancient Catholic world, two main contentions: (1) Thought is free, and (2) The will is *not* free. Let us see what are the results, for by their fruit we shall know them. . . . What are the *necessary* results?—for you cannot live in a world in which the law of gravity rules and yet have water running uphill.

What is the necessary expression of this faith of the modern world?

Let us take the intellectual expression first. It is commonly said, and it is true, that this age is an age of reading, an age of printing. Not to be able to read is the mark of the uneducated—we call such illiterate—they have not *letters*. The written or printed word is the art of arts to-day. Freedom of speech and freedom of the press are taken for granted as the necessary corollary of freedom of thought. Whether or no there can be in fact such a thing as free thought, whether or no there is in fact freedom of speech or freedom of the press (and in some respects it is doubtful whether we have these last), the art of letters is in fact the only

7

art which is free from the trammels of collaboration. Printing may be bad; book production may be worse; but the word I use is exactly the word printed.[1] Whether I have a hand-press or a lino-type machine, it makes no difference to the chosen word.

Is this the state of affairs in any other art you can think of? Every other art demands, for its material expression, the collabora-tion of craftsmen other than the designer.[2] Painting for instance—the painter is dependent on the maker of paints and things to paint on. The musician is dependent upon the maker of instru-ments and persons to use them. The architect is in worst case of all—he is dependent upon a thousand things over which he has little or no control. The printer is hopelessly handicapped—he cannot even get good paper! But the writer—he may say with Pilate, "What I have written, I have written." What is the result? That the art of letters is the only art of our time worth mention-ing. All other arts are either degraded beyond the dreams of Satan or they eke out a miserable and eccentric existence under the care of a few cranks.

The result upon the character of the art of letters is remark-able. The development of the art of writing short stories shows this result very clearly. Subtlety of expression has taken the place of dramatic form. From being a whole history of an adventure (as in the Bayeux Tapestry) the short story has become the micro-scopic exploration of a momentary emotion. Joseph Conrad and Henry James are modern of the moderns. They collaborate with no one—they assume nothing, they depend on nothing but them-selves. The early short story was only half made when it was writ-ten down (and it was very rarely written down at all)—it depended upon the telling—upon the audience—upon the circumstances and surroundings. It was part of the life of men and women—like a dance or a sermon. If the audience was wrong the story was wrong. The modern writer, as such, is divorced from all these

---

[1] Misprints understood.
[2] Except, of course, when the design and execution are the same thing, e.g., a song or a dance which I invent and perform myself.

8

things. What he has written he has written! Is it strange that the character of his art should develop accordingly? Just as landscape painting has gained popularity in exact proportion as the town has destroyed the country and made it impossible for most people to see the sky; just as portrait painting has grown in exact proportion as people worshipped themselves instead of God—there was not such a thing as portrait painting before about the year 1480; so the exact study of our emotions, the microscopic dissection of small portions of things is the natural goal of the modern writer— for he is a man depending solely upon what he can squeeze out of his own soul.[1]

I make no complaint about Conrad or Henry James or even the lesser men who write for money. I say only that such an art as theirs is necessarily the only art which can live unfettered in this time. Every other art is necessarily hampered by its need of the collaboration of many divergent minds. For a work of art to be a success you must have unity—unity of conception, unity of execution. "Very well," says the writer in effect, "I will achieve unity by being alone. . . ." Free thought, then, has achieved this: it has destroyed the unity of Christendom and produced—Thomas Hardy. Thomas Hardy is a great writer—because he has given fine, true, passionate expression to his people. But what is that people? It is a people that knows not Jacob. At the Renaissance man discovered Man and fell down and worshipped. Thomas Hardy has discovered that the face of man is wrinkled and that his eyes are full of tears.

So much for freedom of thought and its intellectual expression.

Now let us discuss the bondage of the will and the necessary expression of that article of faith; for, as H. G. Wells says, "by faith we disbelieve!"

---

[1] Modern painting and sculpture are, of course, though hampered by dependence on materials, pursuing the same course as far as possible. The painter paints pictures independently of any thought of a place where his picture is to go—it is for him nothing but a museum study of his own soul. The sculptor also, divorced from building, is merely a purveyor of emotional self-revelations.

Upon the intellectual side, this is the writer's age, as we have seen. Writing is the only child of our time unspoiled by instrumental delivery! What do we find upon the side of the will? Remember the will is in bondage—there is no free-will. Well indeed have we acted up to this denial! If intellect is concerned with thought, will is concerned with doing and making. What is the right and proper doing and making of slaves? For a slave is one who has no power to execute his will—he is one whom we treat as though he had no free-will.

This is the age of engineering and machinery. Is it not so? Is there not reason to be proud of the achievements of the engineers? Engineering is the typical product of our time. Look at the Forth Bridge. It is the monument, *par excellence,* to our bondage. It is a great monument. It is enormous—it is portentous. And it is the work of slaves. It is the work of men who made no claim to free-will. Even its designer would not claim that he made it such and such a form because so he chose to do it! He would scorn such a foolish idea, and it would be a foolish idea under the circumstances. Engineering deals in necessities, not fancies. And as for the thousands of men who do the actual work of engineering, they are tools—animals with such and such different kinds of manual and intellectual skill or strength. We have denied the freedom of the will. Is it remarkable that we should consciously or unconsciously discover a manner of work and of working compatible with that denial? Surely it is what we should expect. Nor is it engineering, properly so called, which is the only department of our activity showing the same character. Most trades are to-day run upon the same lines. But engineering is the chief because in engineering there is less interference from the idiosyncrasy of individual minds.

We saw that, in the intellectual sphere, the writer of books was alone free from the trammels of collaboration. In the sphere of action (the sphere of the will) the process works the opposite way. In this sphere, free-will being denied, collaboration is no hindrance. Collaboration is the help.

Where you have free-will, collaboration is achieved with difficulty. It is achieved only by voluntary discipline and association as in the mediaeval Guilds—Guilds openly and enthusiastically claiming Religion as their basis and the Church as their protector. But where free-will is denied there is no difficulty about collaboration at all. You simply order iron by the mile, bricks by the thousand, concrete by the ton, and hands by the hundred. There is no more difficulty in obtaining one than the others. Trade unionism does what it can to make labour more expensive but it makes no bones about servility. Your trade union leader is your typical "rationalist"—and rationalism, curiously enough, means free thought and bound will. The trade union leader is not to be blamed. He gets his philosophy ready-made from the very people he is fighting! Nevertheless, as the individual *mind* finds its best expression in the printed word, and the printed word is indeed its only exact expression; so, upon the other hand, the individual *will* is merged, lost, drowned in elaborately subdivided labour. In the typical product of our time, engineering, there is no individual will expressed at all, there is only a collective will, the will of a gang—a gang of slaves.

Here then is a plain issue. We have now reached a period wherein former tendencies are mature. We have now reached a full expression of our modern faith. We can now examine the flower of the tree—for the flower is blowing and will soon show its fruit. It is no longer a question merely of rival doctrines—it is now a matter of rival civilizations.

The position of the artist and the condition of the arts may be made a test. Art is a good test because, by the very nature of the thing, art is that work and that way of working in which man uses his free-will.[1] A civilization based upon the doctrine of free-will naturally and inevitably produces artists—in such a civilization all men are artists and so there is no need to talk about it.

[1] The artist has never denied discipline—he has only demanded that the discipline shall be voluntary as in a religious order or a Guild. "Art is the well-doing of what needs doing" and "a work of art is simply a thing well made." The word "well" is cognate to the word "will" and means made or done agreeably to good will.

11

But a civilization denying free-will naturally and inevitably produces slaves, not artists; and in such a civilization few men are artists, and those few are simply lap-dogs of the rich and a great fuss is made about them!

Of course these facts are belied by appearances. The sepulchre is well white-washed—is not every biscuit box camouflaged to look like a work of art? Is not every house coated with patterned wallpaper—every woman dressed to look pretty? But these things are merely man's attempt to deceive himself—even if the attempt succeed!

But we must beware lest we give the impression that we would return to a Christian civilization for the sake of the art which it naturally produces. Such a motive would be as false as it would be foolish, and as futile as it would be wicked. I have only used art as being the best illustration. The unhealthiness of the tree is shown by its inability to produce a decent flower. But it is not the flower but the fruit for which the gardener works, and the fruit of any civilization is a harvest of souls.

It is often said that a man can be a very good Catholic in a factory—and that is true. Nevertheless, the factory system does not of its nature produce good Catholics, nor is it a system having its roots in Catholicism. It is the system naturally growing out of a philosophy which denies free-will, and which, as a natural consequence, has degraded man to the level of a mere tool.

It is also true, doubtless, that a man can be a very good Catholic and a man of letters. Nevertheless, the men who have pushed the art of writing to its furthest height of subtle expression are not Catholics, and it is to be remembered that that subtlety of expression is the necessary goal in an age in which the working life of the people is degraded by the bondage of industrialism, for in such a bondage the drama of visible life no longer offers the finest subject matter. The Catholic writer is necessarily handicapped, for, even though he be unconscious of the fact, he is unable to divorce himself from the outward life of his time. He can never wholly forget that man is made of matter and spirit, and that both are good. He is not subtly introspective and analytic. Both in the outward and inward life—both in its intellectual expression and in the expression of its will—Catholics are necessarily at war with this age. That we are not more conscious of the fact, that we so often endeavour to make an impossible peace with it— that is the tragedy. You cannot serve God and Mammon.

CHAPTER II

THE LORD'S SONG: A SERMON

Quomodo cantabimus canticum Domini in terra aliena?
How shall we sing the Lord's song in a strange land?

THESE words occur in the one hundred and thirty-sixth psalm
(Vulgate). We are not concerned with the circumstances in which
the Psalm was written or which are described in it. We are only
concerned with the possible application of the words to us now
and here. To sing, and to sing the Lord's song—even if we have
some acquaintance with singing we may easily wonder what song
is the Lord's. The Lord's Prayer we know, but what is the Lord's
song? And what is wrong with our native land that we should
call it strange?

Maybe, darlings and most dear fellow countrymen, if we
knew the Lord we should know his song. *Operatio sequitur esse*;
as one is one does, and if you are a singer you sing. The Lord
then is a singer and first of all his song is a love song. This is
what they mean when they say that the act of creation is a
gratuitous act—that it is a song more pure and purposeless than
even the songs of children and nightingales. For though one may
sing a song for sixpence, it is of the very being of songs that
they may be sung for nothing and are so sung when there are
singers and no sixpences. The Lord is a singer; the work of creation is a song—the morning stars sang together.

And in a song all things must sing. The very words must be

14

musical, the mere syllables. For all is music that is bound. To be free, in the sense of "being on the loose," is alone ugly—deprived of being—like a jellyfish coming undone, disintegrating.

> As music binds into a strict delight
> The manifold random sounds that beat the air. . . .

The service of God is perfect freedom—perfect freedom is to be perfectly bound. God himself is perfectly free—he is perfectly bound to himself—he can be and love nothing but himself. And we are free when we are his, of him and bound to him. And he is a singer. The created universe is a little song of his—a little song, but big enough and loud enough for us—we are notes in it. There is no other explanation of the universe or of us.

The mathematicians have discovered that music can be described in terms of numbers—mournful numbers (life is but an empty dream)—they have not the wit, nor is it their business to discover that mathematics are only intelligible in terms of music,

> one, two, three,
> fiddle-di-dee.

And the mathematicians have recently given us a mathematical exposition of the universe. They have counted the bars and beats in the Lord's little song—so many beats to the minute.

> Hail to thee blithe spirit
> Bird thou never wert—

thou wert never more than a mathematical formula.

But to talk thus is to talk backwards—to offer a chemical analysis of pigments as a description of a picture, to set up the metronome as a critic of music. It is to make economics the only interpretation of history, the acquisition of money the only test of character. It is to make the police the only judge of morals and shopkeepers the only judges of art.

And all these things are done in our time because the first cause is forgotten or denied. It is forgotten or denied that God is Love; that Love must needs sing; that singing is the "characteristic speed" of Love.

15

But perhaps it is not simple forgetfulness: it may be that we are determined not to remember. It is significant that the rising of what we call modern science synchronised with the throwing off of spiritual authority. We have deliberately thrown off the "easy yoke" and "light burden" and have placed ourselves under the hard taskmaster of immutable and impersonal "laws of nature," and this has been done in the name of freedom. A fine freedom we have achieved indeed. In place of a consciousness of personal service, a service of which the common manifestation was song—the very stones sang—we have the consciousness of being nothing in a universal vanity—"the mad folly of the universe rushing from vanity to vanity," as one modern philosopher has felicitously expressed it. The highest virtue we can attempt to claim is a stoical courage in the face of a meaningless concatenation of fortuitous circumstances. Such is the freedom of the sons of science.

This is the strange land in which we find ourselves; a land which is strange because we are not at home in it. We are not at home in it because, though we are conscious of "fair love and of fear and of holy hope," these things not being expressible in arithmetical notation have no place in the land to which we have come.

And among all the people in this strange land they are the more unfortunate who are singers by profession as well as by inclination. How shall they sing the Lord's song in a strange land? A chorister caught in a herd of gibbering monkeys is not more unfortunate. The very noise of his own voice would be drowned in the gibbering and what could they understand if they heard? We have made ourselves a herd of monkeys. We claim descent from monkeys. We deny ourselves the possession of free will—can monkeys have free will? We proclaim the economic interpretation to be the only true interpretation of history—can any other be applicable to monkeys? Can anything but physical need and animal appetite have rule among irrational and mortal beasts? We have set up as our kings those who are most

16

cunning amongst us—most cunning in thieving. Can any virtue but cunning be respectable among monkeys? But we do not call our most cunning men kings; we call them financiers. In this monkeydom the singer is out of place.

But before very long we shall have gone beyond even so high an estate as that of apes. The ideal we now set before ourselves is that of a bee-hive or an ant-heap. The monkey, formerly the man, is to become an insect—a unitary part of a community. Each unit will have its specialised function and all the resources of education-mongers will be enlisted to produce in it the desires and ambitions proper to the function it has to perform. "The station to which I am called" will no longer be one to which I am called by God; it will be a station to which I am commanded by a monster of the imagination called the State. And I shall not so much be commanded, as though I were that imaginary being called a man; I shall be placed here and placed there as being the proper unit for this or that position. My food and clothes will be issued to me in accordance with my needs as a workman; my habitation will be such as experience proves to be necessary to protect me during those hours of sleep in which the battery of my being is recharged for to-morrow's exertion. It has not been observed that bees and ants indulge in play or need to be amused or require any sensual gratifications or satisfactions. As a monkey I spend a great deal too much time in mere foolery and my sensual nature is insatiable. As a bee or an ant I shall have no opportunity for games and no appetite for sensual indulgence. I shall be silent too, and I shall sing no songs.

And if a chorister is unfortunate among monkeys, still more unfortunate will he be among ants. A monkey can at least play the fool; an ant has no notion of play at all. And these are solemn statements. I am not, most dearly beloved, saying things which have no bearing on our life and times. The monkey world is with us. The ant-heap world is the ambition of many of our leaders. The people have ceased to sing; songs and games are the product of specially paid monkeys. And such songs as we thus pay for are no longer the Lord's song. They are not songs of praise; they are not love songs. They are not the songs of Zion. Our fault has been that we sought freedom—we found an iron law of causality. We sought free-thought—we found psychological determinism. We sought free love—we found that we had lost Love itself. Dear silly sheep, we have lost the Shepherd and found only the wolves.

The only freedom we did not seek we have deliberately thrown away. We did not seek for freedom of the will; that was proclaimed as the very corner-stone of human architecture. Upon its possession all men prided themselves, and all law and justice and mercy were founded upon it. Rewards or punishments were not such as we give to cats and dogs for good or bad behaviour. "Well done, good and faithful servant," was not said to animals. "Depart from me, ye cursed" was not said to rabbits. The place prepared for the blessed "by my Father" was not prepared for automatons. Children were not taught by psycho-analysts that they could not help their faults. The sins of the father were visited upon the children but the children were not therefore exonerated from responsibility nor were the dead dishonoured. And this morality of responsibility inevitably pervaded all man's doings. A workman was responsible for his work as much as for his domestic and social acts. This inkpot, this chair, this road, this house, this painted image, this song was good or bad because its maker was good or bad. The bad workman was blamed and the good praised. There were two powers in the land: the spiritual and the temporal. The spiritual lords had power, and were honoured as those who had power over evil spirits and could drive away demons—"and the swine ran headlong into the sea." They had "the words of eternal life." They knew "in whom" we should believe. They prepared us for him "as a bride adorned for her husband." The temporal lords had power and were honoured as men also, knowing the direction of our sailing (for the spiritual lords had told it to them), knew which were fair and which were foul winds. They were men of might whose business it was to defend a physical life with physical strength. Brothers, we all know and it is not necessary to describe the corruptions which befouled both spiritual and temporal powers. Nor is it necessary for us to attempt to apportion the blame. More salutary is it for us to blame ourselves. The sins of our fathers are visited upon us, but we are not therefore helpless or without intelligence. We are not therefore without sin.

But sin is an unpopular word among us. We have thrown away free will. We do not like to be held responsible. We like to be treated as animals, as automatons. When the psychologist says "it is heredity, it is early environment, it is a complex," we applaud. When Augustine says "it is sin," we deride. The word "sin" has become almost meaningless; it has become a sentimental word like "art." To call a thing sinful is considered to be shirking the matter. Sin means nothing to us; it is simply a term of abuse. There is no free will; how can there be responsibility? If a man is not responsible how can he be a sinner? The sinner is he who can do what he knows he should do and does not do it. The sinner is he who can refrain from doing what he knows he should not do and does it. We say there are no such people. We neither know what is right nor have power to act otherwise than as we do. We can be neither blessed nor blamed. We have bodies to be kicked but not souls to be damned. Our liability is not merely limited— it does not exist.

And as the idea of responsibility pervaded all men's works and all their deeds, so does our idea of irresponsibility. We have erected, as is natural, a system of industry exactly corresponding to our philosophy and depending upon it. *Actus sequitur esse.* We do not believe men are responsible; we have made them irresponsible. There is only one power in our world: the power of money. Both spiritual and temporal lords have been driven out; the banker, the stone the builders rejected and often murdered in their anger, has become the head and corner-stone of our architecture. Industry does not exist in order that goods may be abundant, but that the industrialist may be rich. Money is not simply a means for the convenient distribution of good things: it is a means to power; it is power itself. He who has money is king. And this king is not an anointed and sacred person owing allegiance to spiritual overlords and admitting the debt; he is not even the powerful robber who fights with his body for what he possesses. He is the cunning thief, the secret manipulator.

And in the world in which the man of money is king the workman is nothing but a tool. It is common knowledge: the workman is only a tooth on a wheel. What he makes with his hands is not his responsibility and its only concern to his master is its saleability. And as these irresponsible tools are the great majority of the population, they provide the biggest market for the sale of the things they produce. Therefore saleability is that quality in things which makes them attractive to irresponsible tools. By the introduction of machinery the quantity of things made is increased a hundredfold and the responsibility of the workman reduced to nothing. His power to discriminate between good and bad is completely lost and in the end it has necessarily come about that the only things which it is possible to sell are those which no intelligent person finds it possible to buy. *Quomodo cantabimus canticum Domini?*

There is no remedy but that which man alone has power to apply. And every individual must first apply it to himself. He must reclaim the one freedom he has thrown away; and he must throw away all the other freedoms he has falsely claimed. He must reaffirm the freedom of his will and his consequent responsibility for all his deeds and works. He must reaffirm the reality of sin and himself a sinner. Then shall we be free—"with the freedom with which he has made us free." Then shall Babylon be destroyed. Then shall we sing the Lord's Song.

Laus tibi Domine!

CHAPTER III

THE FACTORY SYSTEM
AND CHRISTIANITY

A DISCUSSION OF INCONSISTENCIES

ULTIMATELY any political question is a religious question. A nation which is permeated with evil ideas will inevitably tend to put those ideas into practice and will eventually succeed unless its evil ideas are countered by others. So also a nation which is permeated with good ideas will put those ideas into practice. It is also true that the existence of evil conditions in a country is evidence of the existence of evil ideas in a people; and in a country when bad conditions are prevalent obviously evil ideas must be prevalent. It is therefore necessary, seeing that evil ideas underlie evil conditions, that evil ideas be supplanted by good ideas, for if we spend our energies combating evil conditions without combating the evil ideas underlying them, we can achieve at best palliatives, and do nothing for the salvation of souls, the real object of political activity.

It is true that Governments are, properly, not concerned with ideas but with conditions; but as ideas underlie conditions it is necessary the Governments should be informed, impregnated by ideas. The Church exists for the salvation of souls. Governments exist to create and preserve such conditions as are consistent with the salvation of souls.

If we say that the object of man's existence is man's salvation and that the object of Christianity is to promote man's salvation and that the Church exists to promote Christianity we may go on to say that the only question of any importance in any sphere of activity is whether or no this or that thing is or is not consistent with Christianity.

If for instance I am asked whether or no I believe in machinery I may reply that the question is properly not whether or no I believe in machinery but whether machinery is consistent with Christianity—and obviously machinery as such is consistent with Christianity, though many machines may be used for objects which are inconsistent with Christianity. Christianity is the test.[1]

It is necessary, perhaps, to be clear about the word "consistent" and not confuse it with the word "compatible." For many things are compatible with Christianity which are inconsistent with it. Thus slavery is not incompatible with Christianity but is undoubtedly inconsistent. A man may be a slave or even a slave-master and yet be a Christian, just as a man may be murdered or a murderer and yet be a Christian. A man may even be a good Christian and yet be a slave-owner or a murderer if by some strange chance it has not been brought home to him that slave owning and murder are inconsistent with Christianity; and a man may be a very good Christian and yet be a slave, for though, in the slave, rebellion may be a virtue, for some slaves rebellion is too difficult.

If, then, it be said that such a thing as a Factory or the Factory System is inconsistent with Christianity, it must be clearly understood that that is not saying that a man who works in a factory cannot be a Christian; nor is it saying that a factory owner or one owning shares in a factory or one buying or using things made in a factory cannot be a Christian, for in all these cases the rela-

---

[1] As to what *precisely* is meant by Christianity and the Church and man's salvation, these questions are to be thus answered: Christianity is the Religion of Christ, the Church is the Organisation founded by Him having its visible head in the See of Peter, and man's salvation consists in his happy and charitable union with God in eternal life.

tionship of the soul with God may be good and right and beautiful and the factory is simply a material circumstance the evil of which is not recognized. It is not necessary here to judge of the state of conscience in which men may own factories or work in them or buy their products. Here it is only required to show that it is the system of production called the Factory System that is unchristian. The individual owner or worker may be a Christian under any circumstances—a system is Christian or unchristian by its own nature.

The factory system is unchristian primarily because it deprives workmen of responsibility for their work. A factory "hand" is not responsible for the work he does.

Any workshop in which the workman works simply for his wages and the master simply for his profit is, in essence, that thing called a factory. Factories are generally thought of as large places where many men work. Factories may be quite small places where very few men are employed. Factories are often, or even generally, large places because when workmen are only concerned with wages and masters with profits the small workshop is uneconomical. The Rent and Taxes and working expenses in a small workshop are not in proportion to the size of the place and numbers employed, so that, however willing the workman may be to work in a small shop, the master will always be keen to increase its size and thus enlarge its output and his profits without proportionately increasing his expenses.

The Christian attitude to life and work is that we live and work primarily in order that we may glorify God. The obtaining of the means to go on living is a secondary consideration ("Seek ye *first* the kingdom of God and his justice and all these things shall be added unto you") and the obtaining of profits is, from a Christian point of view, no consideration at all. The labourer is worthy of his hire.

In a factory men simply work for their wages, the masters for their profits, and neither work for the Glory of God.

If a factory hand started thinking about God's glory and began to discover it in his work the whole factory would be put out of gear at once. There is no room for individual fancies of that sort.

Furthermore, just as the factory, for economic reasons, tends to become a large place, so it tends to become a place where labour is divided and subdivided. The division of labour still further reduces the responsibility of the workman and makes absolute the impossibility of his glorifying of God in his work. But division of labour reduces the labour expenses and that is the chief consideration for masters.

The modern factory system is as servile and even more unchristian than the pagan system of slavery. The pagan slave-owner merely owned the slave's body. In the absence of a factory system of workshop organisation the slave's mind was, in practice, his own and the work done by slaves was often of a kind for which each slave was in a high degree actually and personally responsible. The modern factory system is a refinement on the ancient slave system, for in the factory system the workman's mind is owned by the master, while his body is legally free. Thus the Christian tradition of opposition to physical slavery has been dodged and the master has been able to reap all the benefits of slavery without any apparent violation of freedom. But the violation is coming to be recognized on all hands and especially by the workman himself. The so-called "labour unrest" is not, as the masters would have us suppose, entirely due to the unbridled greed of the workmen and their appetite for high wages. It is really due to the workman's instinctive, if inarticulate, desire for freedom and responsibility and if it chiefly takes the form of a demand for higher wages and shorter hours, this is only a case of "the biter bit," for higher profits and longer holidays is the chief ambition of the masters. The worship of money is a worship which the workman has learned from his superiors.

Now there are two lines of opposition to arguments such as these. On the one hand are those who, while agreeing that the factory system is in many respects unwholesome, say that by a proper system of "scientific management" all the evils of factory work can be done away with. On the other are those who, disregarding any real or imaginary objections to factory life and work, are so obsessed by the notion that the populations of the modern world could not be fed and clothed and housed by any other system than that of factories that they regard as mere foolishness any suggestions for a return to production by small workshops owned by individual workmen and worked by them with a few assistants and apprentices. The one kind says: we see the evil but it can be remedied by "scientific management," the other kind says: evil or no evil—the factory system is essential to the modern world.

There is no need to argue here about the remedy proposed by those who advocate "scientific management" nor to argue with those who talk about large populations. They have great possessions and are pretty sure to turn away sorrowful. Our only concern is to discover the truth that the modern system of production is evil. If that be admitted the remedy is obvious.

It is a Christian principle that every individual soul is responsible and not irresponsible. It is Christian teaching that the first human activity is the love of God and the glorifying of Him. It is not sufficient that God be glorified by faith; it is equally necessary that He be glorified by works. The modern system of factory production deprives men of the power to glorify God in their works and of the responsibility for so doing. Therefore the Factory System is evil and damned. And just as Slavery, being discovered to be inconsistent with Christianity, was gradually destroyed by Christians, so the Factory System, being discovered to be servile and therefore inconsistent with Christianity, will be gradually destroyed by Christians.

Laus tibi Christe! Vade Satanas!

NOTE 1. S. Thomas Aquinas says (Summa, I^a, Q. 96, Art. 4): "Liber est causa sui, servus autem ordinatur ad alium." This is to say: The freeman is responsible for himself, but for the slave another is responsible.

NOTE 2. The various schemes of co-operation between masters and men—"profit sharing," "combined management," etc.—make no attempt to attack the problem at its root. They are merely attempts to stay the discontent of the workers and they are bound to fail; for the real, though as yet unexpressed, cause of discontent is not lack of money, but lack of responsibility. Just as slavery is wrong, however well treated the slaves—so factory production is wrong, however well paid the hands. Factory production is wrong because it is production for profit and because it deprives the workman of responsibility. Even "combined management" must fail, in spite of its presumed gift of partial responsibility to the men, because there still remains in the combination one party, that of the masters, whose interests are primarily the making of profits, and those interests are bound to clash with those of the men, for the men are first of all workmen and not financiers and the interests of workmen have since the beginning of the world been different from, and opposed to, those of buyers and sellers.

APPENDIX

The Factory System is unchristian because:

It puts the service and glory of man before the service and glory of God.

It promotes the comfort of man and destroys the worship and praise of God.

It puts the making of money before the making of goods.

It puts quantity before quality—for quantity can be determined by measurement, whereas quality demands imagination and cannot be measured.

It deprives the workman of responsibility for his work.

It is subject only to "efficient causes" and not to "final causes."

It depends upon the notion that "it is more blessed to receive than to give."

It destroys the personal relationship of maker to buyer.

It promotes the war of classes (masters *versus* men).

It prevents Trades Unions from becoming Trades Guilds.

It promotes the notion that leisure time is more to be desired than work time, for it deprives the workman of any power to express his own ideas in his work or to get any amusement out of it, thus causing him always to look forward to the time when he will stop work.

It flatters the consumer to capture his custom, and covers the land with damnable advertisements.

It subdivides labour so that a workman becomes merely a tool.

It puts a premium upon mechanical dexterity and a discount upon intellectual and spiritual ability in the workman.

It undermines the family, for it drags both men and women into its net and destroys home work and home life.

It depends upon militarism, for without the support of the military the system would have been destroyed in its beginnings and the strike is only rendered abortive because in the last resort the soldiers can be brought out to shoot down the strikers.

It promotes wars, for its destroys local markets and makes trade dependent upon "world markets" and financial magnates. Over-production is inevitable and when there is over-production there must be a struggle for fresh markets.

CHAPTER IV

DAVID JONES

WHEN one starts writing about things, it seems inevitable that one should see them in terms of categories, especially when, as at present, schools and rumours of schools are on every hand; and though the general notion precedes the particular notion, and "Man starts with the highest type of knowledge—the intuition of pure Being," nevertheless, now that the Royal Academy is not only Royal but commonplace, we must make our first category that of purely naturalistic painting.

Let us say then that first of all there is the painting which sets out to be an exact representation or record of something seen by the painter, and as he sees it. Regarded as serving the useful function of making records of things deemed worth recording, this kind of painting is by no means despicable; and when the artist's aim is sufficiently simple-minded, it may even result in paintings of more than historic value. The drawings of Ruskin of plants and animals, because Ruskin was so intensely interested in the plant or animal he was drawing and was not concerned with anything else, and many Dutch Interiors, are excellent works of art in their kind, and that kind is in itself a good one. It is only when the aim of the artist is impure and he allows himself to be sidetracked by irrelevant considerations that we get such degradations as Luke Fildes and the ordinary run of Royal Academy painters, whose work is not a failure because of any lack of technical ability, but simply because it lacks purity of motive. It is devoid of any single-minded enthusiasm.

And it is not only *things* which provide the painter with that saving grace of single-mindedness; for it now appears clearly that the real beauty of the works of the best French impressionists is of the same kind as that achieved by the Pre-Raphaelites; but where Holman Hunt painted faithful representations of objects of domestic and social affection inspired by Victorian sentiment and romanticism the Frenchmen made faithful representations of the light before their eyes, inspired by Rousseauish and equally romantic worship of Nature.

At the other end of the categoric pole is purely abstract painting, and here there is no question of representation or imitation. But as the creature called man is not of a kind which can make pure inventions—he cannot create out of nothing—even his most abstract efforts have some kind of derivation from things seen and known.

Everybody knows that mere patterns are delightful and there is no need to inquire about their origins. It is only for catalogue purposes that we label this pattern the "Egg and Dart," or that the "Sponge Bag." But there comes a point at which patterns cease to be "mere"; they even arrive at a place where they seem to merit such high-sounding adjectives as profound and grand and sublime.

It is this discovery which has given life to much of the revolt against the sentimental naturalistic painting of the last three hundred years, and critics have gone so far as to affirm that this quality of form is the one which gives value even to those paintings in which the subject matter is the most obvious.

"Significant Form"—that is the cry! God and Love, the story of Creation and Redemption, domestic bliss, or human adventure, all these things, from this point of view, are seen to be merely vehicles for what is pleasing formally. And not only does the modern painter of this school of thought set out to make paintings which shall make no appeal to sentimental or anecdotal interest, but ancient paintings have been revalued. Rubens is no longer a painter of goddesses, or Raphael even of Madonnas. Such things are now considered irrelevant to the professional artist; it is the formal aspect of their work which alone gives them their value, and much good has been done in this revaluation, for many reputations precariously balanced upon mere social approbation have been permanently destroyed. Nevertheless, such an exclusive insistence upon form, however useful it has been as an eye-opener, is as essentially heretical as a too-exclusive insistence upon representative veracity, or upon utility, i.e., the value of a painting as doing something of service to its owner; for heresy in artistic thinking, as in other matters, is little more than a running amok after one statement of the truth to the exclusion of others. Many a painting whose producer thought of nothing but verisimilitude and the service of his fellow-men, does indeed achieve what Mr. Clive Bell calls "Significant Form." Many a painting whose producer thought of nothing but formal values does indeed achieve even verisimilitude and serviceableness. Nevertheless, the truth is in neither one nor the other; it emerges clearly that the Golden Rule is not a mean between extremes but a combination of the two. Reality, the Kingdom of Heaven, is neither merely useful nor merely amusing; man is neither merely material nor merely spiritual, and art, though, by definition, concerned solely with the good of the work to be made, is concerned with work to be made for men. The too purely prudential attitude of the Victorians, the too purely artistic attitude of the moderns, both alike miss the reality.

The modern artist is therefore as much in difficulties as his predecessor. In saying that the subject of a picture does not matter and that a picture should look as well upside down as the right way up (that, in fact, there is no right way up), he is saying something just as erroneous as the old-fashioned art master who talked of nothing but anatomical exactitude and anecdotal or romantic interest. But to get the matter right again unfortunately requires either quite exceptional clear-headedness as a gift of nature, or guidance from an authority which is not subject to heretical leanings, and this is no part of any art training but is a matter of philosophy and religion.

Mr. David Jones is a painter who sees this modern dilemma very clearly, and we should miss all the quality of his work if we did not see that it is a combination of two enthusiasms, that of the man who is enamoured of the spiritual world and at the same time as much enamoured of the material body in which he must clothe his vision. The difficulty of preserving a balance between representative felicities and those which are purely intellectual and aesthetic is perhaps greater for painters than any other kind of artist. Verisimilitude, though perhaps not easy in any art, is easier in painting than in most, especially when four centuries of concentration upon it by artists and the illustrated press have flooded the world with photographic representations. The imitation of natural appearance, if it ever was a difficulty, is difficulty no longer. Of course, it requires hard work and obedience to the rules to become proficient, but these are difficulties which determination can overcome. The real difficulty now lies in making a rebellion which shall be neither an affair of archaism nor of charlatanism. The painter must have a very clear idea as to what a picture really is, and as to why and what he really likes painting. And not only must the painter thus clear his head, but he who buys and he who criticizes are under the same obligation. The most clear-headed and enthusiastic painter may fail to win any support unless those who see his work are capable of sharing or sympathizing with his aims.

David Jones was born at Brockley in Kent in 1895. He was a student under A. S. Hartrick, at the Camberwell School of Art, from 1910 to 1914. He served throughout the war with the Royal Welch Fusiliers. From 1919 to 1921 he was a student, under Walter Bayes, at the Westminster School of Art. Apart from a few small sculptors in boxwood (things which alone would place him in the first rank of modern artists), his work has been chiefly wood and copper engraving, and water-colour drawing. He has done engravings for the St. Dominic's Press, the Golden Cockerel

Press ("Gulliver," "Jonah," "The Deluge") and for Douglas
Cleverdon, Bristol ("The Ancient Mariner"). Of the last it may
be said that Coleridge's poem has for the first time found adequate
pictorial accompaniment. As a water-colourist he has worked
chiefly in Wales, the south of France, at Hove and at Brockley.
Though in one place he may find more inspiration than another,
it is not places that most concern him. What concerns him is the
universal thing showing through the particular thing, and as a
painter it is this showing through that he endeavours to capture.
The eye sees particular things, but the man's delight in the physical vision is checked by the mind's apprehension of the universal
informing it. Nevertheless, in spite of this idealistic attitude he
never loses sight of the fact that it is a painting he is making—or
a drawing, or an engraving; it is not merely an essay in Platonic
research. Paper and paint, the brush, the graver all make their
own proper demands and yield their own proper fruits. The
difficulty, the job, is one of translation—how to translate this universal thing into terms of paint and paper.

What starts a man painting, why this physical concern for
spiritual things? It must on no account be supposed that David
Jones is that kind of "high-brow" whose essays in paint are a
condescension. Paint, colour, flowers, flesh, these are the things
which delight him. But his is that kind of fastidiousness which is
not content with simple reproductions of delightful things. Even
"the particularly juicy bit" which starts him off he holds with a
grasp which at any moment he is prepared to relinquish. And
yet, and yet—even though the grasp be relinquished, the thing
and its delightfulness still pervade and must pervade the painting.

To David Jones, a painting is neither simply a representation
nor simply a painted pattern. He resists equally firmly the seduc-
tion in either direction. If he delights especially in the beauty of
flowers and animals and young girls, his paintings are not therefore to be regarded simply as records of those things; there is
nothing of the Pre-Raphaelite in him. If he delights in the purely
aesthetic quality of paint on paper, the beauty of arabesque, of

light and of colour, his paintings are not therefore simply essays in abstraction. He is not an Impressionist, nor, except by accident of date, a Post-Impressionist. It is not for me to say simply that his work is good; my object is rather to make a clear statement of his point of view, so that those who see his work will at least be in the position to judge fairly, and will not be in the position of those unfortunate persons who, having paid to see a football match, find a cricket match inflicted upon them.

CHAPTER V

CLOTHING WITHOUT CLOTH

AN ESSAY ON THE NUDE

THE distinction between art and nature leads to much confusion. That there are two things, as there are two words, may be taken for granted, but where one begins and the other ends is a question not easily answered. Many things lightly called art are as natural as sky and sea, and of all the natural things commonly supposed to be works of art nothing is more natural than clothes.

The real distinction between art and nature is between those things which are the product of deliberate and voluntary acts and those that are done without thought and without consent. Between the two there is the innumerable multitude of things which people do and make without *full* deliberation and *more or less* involuntarily. How many human acts are fully deliberate and fully willed? Examination discloses that it is exceedingly difficult to prove any act as being either, for most human acts are partly compelled by appetite or by fear and are hardly deliberated at all. Such a condition of things may be lacking in dignity, but it is not therefore in the least blameworthy or despicable. It would be a terrible nuisance if we had to digest our food on purpose, and to have to think out everything for ourselves and consider the rights and wrongs of it would not only be a very lengthy business, but one far beyond our mental capacities. Nevertheless a certain amount of deliberation is the accompaniment of most human action, and consequently we may assume that neither appetite nor fear is always in complete control.

It may be difficult to say what Nature is, for Nature interpenetrates everything. To produce works of art is natural to men, therefore works of art are, in a sense, themselves natural objects. Nature, the natural world, we must suppose to be the product of the fully deliberate will of God, therefore the natural world is itself a work of art. But though, in this apparent confusion, the definition of nature remains obscure, the thing called art emerges clearly. Art is skill; that is what it has always been and what it has always been said to be. But it is a deliberate skill; and a work of art is the product of voluntary acts directed towards making. Hence art is a virtue of the intelligence—it is of the mind. Deliberation and volition are essential to the thing called Art. An involuntary act or an act performed without intellection may be good or bad *in se;* it is not the act of an artist.

Now clothes are supposed to be works of art. There is, as is well known, the art of the dressmaker, there is the art of the tailor, "the Sartorial Art," and the business of making costumes for wear in the theatre is obviously a thing of high artistic importance. But there are also the art of the hairdresser and the art of making up. The lip-stick and the powder-puff may be used with deliberation and not always with malice. At once the business of human appearance is seen to be concerned not with clothes only but with the human skin and hair also. Doing your hair—if only scraping it off—is a part of dressing, and clothes may be as thin as paint and powder. A man without clothes may be supposed to be simply a man without coat or trousers, a naked woman may be thought of as one without a skirt; but the business of dressing obviously does not stop at garments of such mere utility, nor does it stop when all manufactured garments have been put on or taken off. There is no escape from the conclusion that skin and hair are themselves garments to be treated well or ill, and that one may be naked and yet not necessarily undressed.

The natural, for man, is what he does without deliberation

and with the simple consent of appetite or fear. What you do because you want to or because you are afraid not to, what you do without thinking out the *pros* and *cons*—those things are, for man, natural acts. And clothing himself is among such acts. Let us begin at the beginning. The baby does not wear clothes deliberately and with full consent. The baby wears clothes simply because the parents put them upon him. Nor do the parents deliberate about it or consider whether they will or will not withhold their consent. They accept without question the law which lays it down that boy babies shall have blue ribands and girl babies pink. They give the baby his loin cloth to save themselves trouble, without a moment's consideration of the complexes they are causing; and you could hardly get them to deliberate about it if you tried. To keep the baby warm and to hide its carelessness are natural acts. To wear clothes is natural to babies; without them they are cold and horrid. And what is begun in the cradle is continued throughout the subsequent years of childhood and adolescence. Boys and girls use no deliberation whatever about it, and even if they do not particularly *desire* clothes, they are afraid to be without them. The desire for clothes comes with maturity, but the fear of nakedness is not lost. Even when good behavior has long since displaced the carelessness of the cradle the complex remains, and the confusion of youth, not knowing whether organs of sex are despicable because of their proximity to organs of drainage or organs of drainage venerable by reason of their proximity to organs of sex, makes simple fear into a complicated emotion of shame and modesty.

Moreover, and quite apart from the sex and sanitation business, there is the question of warmth; and even among animals clothing of skin and hair is sometimes insufficient. All horses follow much the same profession or occupation, but even among horses the clothes question is of importance. The harness of cart horses is *naturally* different from that of carriage horses, and the rug suitable for my pony is *naturally* unsuitable for a Derby winner. How much more is the difference between the clothes suitable for me and those suitable for you! It is *natural* for a miner to wear different clothes from those worn by a "Lady of fashion." A parcel of left-off clothes sent to either by the other would be discarded without any deliberation whatever. Appetite would be insufficient to overcome fear, and the unsuitability would be obvious. Yet it is possible to deliberate even about so natural a thing as clothes, and it is possible to conclude, without any surrender of man's natural rationality, that our clothes of skin and hair are sometimes sufficient and sometimes even more suitable than those of cotton, silk or wool with which in a certain sense we are born.

Assuming, gratuitously enough, that by clothes we mean the artificial integuments which we manufacture for ourselves, the notable thing about man is not that he wears clothes—he does that, as all animals do, without deliberation and without any but simple consent: the notable thing is not that he sometimes uses deliberation as to cut and colour—that follows naturally from his rational nature; the notable thing about man is that he deliberately takes clothes off. As an animal he wears clothes; it is only as man that he can deliberately go naked.

But to do a thing deliberately means to do it with some show of reason. What reason can there be for nakedness? There are all sorts of reasons. There is the reason of HUMILITY; as when men cut off their flowing beards and go about with naked chins. So also, in countries that are not too cold, the man who would be really holy, or thought of as such, puts away all the aggrandizement of tailorings and sits humbly naked by the roadside; and the command to clothe the naked is not a command to impose finery upon people, but a condemnation of those who would impose humility on us against our wills. And if the nakedness of humility does not commonly extend to the disclosure of sex, that is because even among saints the babyhood complex is generally still unresolved, and sex still remains uniquely significant.

There is probably no escape from this nor need to wish for one. If we consider our bodies it is immediately clear that of all

our limbs and organs those by which we are known as he or she
are peculiar in having a relation to others beside ourselves. You
may like my eyes or my shoulders, my hair or my hands, but it is
a disinterested appreciation, you do not want them for yourself.
If you dislike them it is me you chiefly pity; you are glad you are
not like me, but it makes little difference to you. It is otherwise
with sexual things. Sex organs do not exist simply for him who
has them but for her also who has them not. Love is neither blind
nor irrational, and, as the talk of lovers shows, it is their sex and
not themselves that they surrender to one another. Who would
wish to escape from this? The exposure of sex is not simply the
exposure of what is mine but also the exposure of what is yours
or another's. And this is not merely a matter of possessiveness or
the guarding of private possessions: it is, and quite apart from
childish complexes and adolescent confusion, an intuitive and traditional regard for what is of social as well as private significance.

I ask again: Who would wish it otherwise? The whole trouble
is to preserve a balance between what is good in itself and what
is good in relation to other things—between absolute and relative.
An excessive regard for what is good in itself may lead either to a
barren intellectualism or a frigid indifference. An excessive regard for what is good only in its proper relations may lead to all
sorts of unwholesome mystery-mongerings. The lily needs no
gilding and the mystery of sex need not be made more mysterious.
On the other hand the beauty of the virile member in itself, of
breasts or of full rounded buttocks, is not independent of their
sexual significance.

In any essay on nakedness sexual display is the crux of the
matter. Apart from that there is little difficulty. If legs be sexually
attractive or significant, then the display of legs is sexual display.
If bare shoulders invite consideration of bare breasts, then bare
shoulders are sexually inviting. If tight trousers make maleness
prominent then tight trousers are more than a matter of private
convenience. But such questions demand more than police argument. Too much mysterious hiding leads to as much disorder as

too much nakedness. Right thinking is even more important than good conduct; for good conduct is only good because it is the fruit of good sense.

But bare bodies or tight-fitting clothes are secondary matters compared with the actual uncovering of sex organs; and here we are confronted not by what is provocative but by the provocation itself—not what is suggestive but by the thing suggested. Here again more than the logic of the policeman is required, even here as much harm can be done by improper secrecy as by improper exhibition; even here good conduct must be the fruit of right thinking, and it must at least be admitted that though and even *because* the general rule be that sex organs be hidden there are, and are *therefore,* occasions when they are rightly displayed. Between wedded lovers there can be no question about it; all other places and occasions are matters of public politics. If prudery (and the wantonness of which it is commonly the cloak or the accompaniment) be rampant, let there be naked bathing in parks. If sexual frigidity be rampant, let nakedness be restricted, for clothes are the best aphrodisiac. But prudes cannot decide who are wantons, nor can wantons decide who are prudes.

And in painting and sculpture the same considerations apply. Speaking generally all public exhibition of naturalistic representations is improper. In former times, when this fact was better realized, the art of portraiture did not even exist. If the public exhibitions of naturalistic painting and sculpture—even of faces and landscapes—tends to impropriety (because it is embarrassing in its revelation of the personality of the artist) it is obvious that the public exhibition of naturalistic representations of sex is more indecent. The revelation of the absolute good is never indecent—the danger here is of over-intellectualism and sexual frigidity. The revelation of the relative good, of that which though good in itself is also good for you, is generally indecent except as a joke (e.g., in lampoons or caricatures) or in private (e.g., in the home or in bed); in fact naturalism is only saved from impropriety by being funny or secret. But the occasions for fun are many and the definition of secrecy should be wide. Jokes were broader, and prudery less, in times when conventional art was widespread and before Puritanism had destroyed the hieratical conception of married love; for those things which are more venerable lend themselves to comic treatment only when their venerable nature is known and understood. "It is funnier to have a nose than to have a Roman nose," but it is not funny to have sex, though the best jokes are made about it, and that is just the difference. And the jokes will be as flat as ditchwater unless the awful seriousness of the subject be appreciated. Naturalistic art is always as indecent as it is technically absurd; and the naturalistic representation of sex is more indecent than anything else because more embarrassing and socially disordinating.

Conventional art, on the other hand, is decent, but the convention must be more than a technical one. A work of art has its origin in the mind, the mind is the arbiter, not the tool or the stone. The mind lays down *what*, the stone only says *how*. If the mind says "hair," the stone says such and such a way of doing hair is appropriate to stone. If the mind says "round thighs," the stone says such and such a way of working will produce roundness best. And as the work should be according to convention so also should be the occasion. Bathing-suits in banks are no less ridiculous than sleeping-suits in churches. Bare bellies in the street are no less silly than spats under bedclothes, and what is true of living bodies applies also to bodies of stone. But here the conventions are necessarily different; for a naked man of stone is different from one of flesh and blood (unless the art of the sculptor be prostituted to the production of illusions; in which case the rules are the same for both and the work of sculpture suitable only for exhibition in private or at the gallery of Madame Tussaud). A naked man in stone is not only a naked man: it is also a stone man—a man as he should be in stone. And this does not only imply that the technique of stone carving imposes limitations upon naturalism (though it does indeed do so, and naturalistic carvings are generally technically absurd and consequently generally unpleasant);

the implication is also that it is not possible to think of a man in stone without considerations of public relations—place and purpose. A man carved in stone is not conventionalized only because the stone imposes conventions, but also—and even more imperatively—because place and occasion impose them. It is not only in matters of sexual presentation that these things apply. A naturalistic portrait of a public man, or even of his horse, is indecent in a public place (the only place where it would not be so is a cupboard in his wife's bedroom). Public display should be confined to what is of public importance. The exact shape of a man's eyebrows is no more a public concern than that of any other thing he possesses. And the streets and public buildings are not the only public places. The drawing-room mantelpiece is not entirely private; naturalistic display is only suitable and endurable in private places.

Apart from naturalistic art which, as I have said, is absurd except as an absurdity, the value of works of art is an intrinsic value: they are good things in themselves. But they are also symbols. What do they symbolize? If they symbolize what is good in itself and good for us, then only prudery would condemn painted sexual organs as such. If they symbolize what is bad, only wantons would want them. One thing only in the whole world is more absurd than the convention of the fig leaf, and that is the pretence that sex is not uniquely significant.

A convention is a coming together—an agreement between *minds;* it is not a thing got out of a dictionary of ornament. What do we agree about sex? Is our general agreement to hide it founded upon delight in its significance or upon puritanical disgust and Manichaeism? Do women of to-day show their legs because they have risen superior to the prudery of their grandmothers, or is it because, in a world in which two women out of every ten cannot possibly find husbands, and polygyny is taboo, a display of their limbs gives them an advantage? Is it because the supply of cheap contraceptives makes them no longer afraid, or is it simply sexual indifference? Who shall say? If we could suddenly reverse the numerical proportions of men and women, or remove the taboo on polygeny, or destroy all knowledge of contraception; if we could probe their minds and discover their pruderies and frigidities, we might be able to answer. Meanwhile, the most we can do is to encourage reasonable deliberation and discipline, and the advertisement of the only venerable Authority.

But, apart from this local confusion, the world-wide convention of sexual modesty, that is to say the world-wide agreement to cover the organs of sex, is founded upon the world-wide realization, whether stately or not, that sex is of social significance—necessarily, essentially and always. What we call "private parts" are kept private because their public display is provocative of social disorder. Modesty is not derived from the possession of what is shameful but of what is good; but it is a social, a public good, and it is its unwarranted display that is shameful. The desire of men and women for one another is good (none but the foolish would wish it lessened), but its stimulation is rarely necessary. Their possession of one another is glorious, delightful, heavenly and blessed (none but bad men deny this); but on account of its significance and consequences, it must be sanctified. Broadly speaking, sexual display, except under suitable circumstances, can only be supported on a basis of sexual contraception (and that is essentially a denial of the primary significance of the sexual act), or on a basis of sexual frigidity (and that is not emancipation but decadence). Adam sinned when he fell from Contemplation. His consequent disobedience led to a Babel of confusion. The solution is a return to obedience in order that we may return to Contemplation.

In addition to the reason of humility, CONVENIENCE is a reason for nakedness. In many kinds of games artificial integuments are a hindrance not merely to the proper playing but also to the proper enjoyment of the game. But places and seasons have their bearings on this; and though bathing in the sea—when it is not chiefly parading on the beach—is always better and more enjoyably done completely naked, dancing on the grass can only be done without clothes when the weather is warm. Here a general rule may be suggested: As regards the players, nakedness is not sexually provocative if they are sufficiently used to it, and as regards the spectators, nakedness is not sexually provocative if they are also on occasion players. But two things must be remembered; that what is sexually provocative to one person may be less so or not at all to another, and that sex stimulation is not always and invariably wrong. Whether it be wrong for *you* is for you and your Doctor to judge; whether it be wrong in public places is for Doctors and Princes to establish—and by Doctors I mean those authorized to *teach*.

Moreover, there are many degrees of nakedness, and pleasure is primarily of the mind. To go barefooted and bareheaded would seem a considerable indecency to a city banker and not in the least enjoyable; to wear an overcoat at lunch is probably indecent in the Travellers' Club. Sun and wind and showers are very pleasant on the naked body, but would not be so if, by accident, one appeared thus at a garden party or on a military parade ground. And this is not at all because our clothes of skin and hair are in themselves shameful; but because it is ridiculous, and therefore unenjoyable, and therefore indecent to take clothes off on those occasions when reason more particularly demands that we shall put them on, or to put them on when we should take them off.

Another reason for nakedness is PLEASURE pure and simple. For the beautiful thing is that which being seen pleases, and nothing is more pleasing when seen than the nude human body clothed in its variously tinted skin, decked out with its four or five bushes of hair, modelled more subtly than is any other creature for movement and strength, from which shines out the unique radiance of rationality. The soul is the *form* of the body, as they discovered in the Lyceum and proclaimed in the Universities (its *form*, i.e., not its *shape* but that which *informs* it); and as the beauty of bones is a functional beauty—the radiance of that which is truly suitable for its function (and such is the beauty of trees and flowers, of beetles and battleships, of animals and machines;

43

though the beauty of those things is, for men, partly imputed to them by the goodness of our associations with them), so the beauty of man's body is the radiance of a rational being. It has functional beauty also and no lack; but man's function is more than physical. His body's beauty is not simply that of a creature admirably adapted for running—many other animals outrun him, but he can run well enough. He is not as strong as the lion or as nimble as the monkey. If he would fly he must manufacture his wings. Man's function is that of lord and master of all other creatures, child of God, inheritor of the Kingdom of Heaven. Remembering only our race of shopkeepers, we have forgotten these things.

Clothes are natural and proper to man. Clothes are not primarily for warmth or convenience or even for modesty. Clothes are primarily for dignity and adornment. But all men have not the same dignity. The dignity of the apprentice is different from that of his master and the dignity of kings is different from that of shepherds—whether of sheep or of men. And adornment has its different uses and occasions; it may either be suitable to my state or simply the legitimate expression of my personal fancy. But the human body, unclothed and even unkempt, though lacking all the panoply of dignity and ornament, is a kind of generalization. The naked man is neither king nor courtier, labourer nor merchant, soldier nor citizen, rich nor poor, professor nor student, lay nor cleric: he is simply man, *Homo Sapiens,* noble or ignoble, that and nothing else.

CHAPTER VI

JOHN RUSKIN

(An address at the English Speaking Union, 8 Feb. 1934)

WHEN I was told that I was going to be called upon to speak this evening, I had to consider how it seemed to me—this question of Ruskin and the world, and as I thought about it, I had a sort of vision in which I saw upon the walls of all the offices in the city during the nineteenth century the text, "Thou God seest me." Fortunately for men of business, such a text leaves it extremely vague as to what God is, and so they were able to recline upon the words of the Psalmist, "I have been young, and now am old; yet have I not seen the righteous forsaken, nor his seed begging bread." In the absence of any test as to what is good, business men were able to assure themselves that if things paid, they must be good. The righteous was never seen begging his bread; therefore success in business was the test of the good. The right thing was what paid. The righteous man was the successful business man.

That is the modern world, in which all things are merchandise, in which buyers and sellers are rulers, in which the money market eventually supersedes even the buyers and sellers, and finally the banks become the bosses. The banks do indeed rule.

But now I see before me on this wall the text, "Thou Ruskin seest me." I am remembering John Ruskin. If men of business had had that text upon their walls, it would have been of much more avail than the text they had.

Ruskin was chiefly thought of as an art critic, and so long as he kept to that straight and narrow way, all was well. But, unfortunately for him, he saw life more or less whole. He saw—no one else did, or very few—that art and life were bound together. He saw, he foresaw, what we now see, the complete divorce of art from life which industrialism entails.

On the one hand there are the artists (painters, sculptors, poets, musicians), more and more concerned with introspection, more and more concerned with digging about in their own souls to discover peculiar emotions, the special emotions of special people —eccentric people necessarily become more and more eccentric as they become more and more isolated—eventually having the museum for their one resting place. (I have heard modern artists in conversation many times congratulate themselves upon the fact that such and such a work of theirs has been bought by Manchester, or Edinburgh, or Melbourne. That is what modern art works are for. The museum is their home.)

On the other hand we see all the ordinary needs of life produced by commercial production—the machine, mass production. All things are thought of by their makers simply as things to be sold. The ordinary workman is reduced to a subhuman condition of intellectual irresponsibility. The man is now a tool, a tooth on a wheel, depending for his amusement on what is served out to him in his spare time. They say that culture is the produce of leisure. Those who now enjoy the leisure of unemployment receive the culture which the B.B.C. is able to supply, lectures on this and that. Their work is no longer their means to culture.

On the one hand we see the artist more and more solely concerned with his own interior life; on the other hand, the workman less and less concerned with what he makes and only "living" when he is not working.

You may think all is well. Ruskin did not. "Thou Ruskin seest me." I speak with diffidence because I rather fancy in some sort of way he may be seeing me, and hearing me, and I am very much afraid. I am wondering whether I am really saying the truth about him.

But I believe that though Ruskin's ideas on religion were full of prejudices and full of pruderies, and though his ideas on art were full of pedantry and false reasoning—as, for instance, when he described architecture as being that kind of building to which some sort of sculpture was added, as though architecture could not exist without sculpture (that is putting it rather crudely, I know, but that was the gist of his ideas)—though such were his ideas upon religion and art, his ideas on justice and equity, founded less upon idiosyncrasy, are unshakable and permanent.

If Ruskin is to be remembered for one thing only, I suggest that he is to be remembered for one book, the book called *Unto this Last,* and, of course, the same ideas scattered about in many of his lectures and other writings. All he said about Gothic, about painting, can go as comparatively worthless compared with his *Unto this Last.* He is to be remembered as one of the few men of the nineteenth century who saw clearly that the roots of human action, and therefore of human art, are moral roots.

Morris saw the evils of modern industrial conditions, but he could see no remedy but the short cut of a certain kind of politics. Ruskin saw the evil, and he saw its real roots; hence the contumely with which he was greeted. The art critic should leave ethics and economics alone.

To some extent the business man worships art (especially when he is persuaded that it is a good investment), but you must not interfere with trade. Well, they have made a fine mess of it with their trading and finance. Let us remember Ruskin as the man who foretold their doom.

CHAPTER VII

ALL ART IS PROPAGANDA

(A contribution to 5 *on revolutionary art, published in 1935)*

IN the confusion of our time few things are more uncertain than the relations between art and life. On the one hand we have the high and lifted-up exponents of "pure" art (industrialism has released the artist from the necessity of making anything useful). On the other we have people who say: all things made are works of art; all art is commercial art (for commerce is the business of exchanging things and no painter can eat a picture so he must exchange it for bread); machine-made things are works of art (for someone had to design them and superintend their making, and to use a machine, however elaborate, is simply to use an elaborate kind of tool—the machine-minders being simply parts of the machinery); all art is politically significant (for nothing can be made which does not contribute, in small ways or big, to the order or disorder of society); and so, of course, all art is propaganda because, whether the artist is conscious of it or not, there is nothing he can do but must have propaganda value, that is to say value for or against one cause or another.

The paintings and sculptures and architectural designs exhibited at the Royal Academy every year express the "values" of the dominant class. Therefore, they are propaganda for the successful bourgeois.

Of course the painter doesn't say to himself: now I'm going

to do a spot of propaganda for the idle rich. He'd be ashamed to. So he has to wrap himself in art jargon instead, and talk about another kind of values—"tone values," "formal relations," the "relations of masses," and so his work becomes propaganda for *studio* values.

Confronted by innumerable contradictory religions and philosophies, none of which compels his assent or claims his service, the artist is thrown back on the specialities of the studio; aided and abetted by art critics and connoisseurs, he ends by thinking that they alone are art, and so art, having no connection with meaning, seems to have no connection with propaganda. Art and propaganda are held to be mutually exclusive terms and to say such and such is propaganda is to say it is a bad work of art.

The fact remains. All art is propaganda, for it is in fact impossible to do anything, to make anything, which is not expressive of "value." The artist may say he does not care who likes his work or dislikes it, whether it effects anything or not, but directly he shows his work to anyone, and more so if he shows it in a public place, he becomes a responsible propagandist for the "values," the ethos, expressed in his work and therefore promoted by it.

There is no escape from this. The artist cannot escape being a man. He cannot escape responsibility, he cannot escape being a propagandist.

But there is not generally any need to talk about it.

It is only necessary to recognize the fact, and it is specially necessary to-day because both the art critics, at one end of the pole, and the complacent bourgeoisie, at the other, are united in trying to make art meaningless, to keep the artist in the studio, to regard him simply as an entertainer.

Am I saying that a Catholic novelist has got to have his creed sticking out on every page of his book so that people can use it instead of the Penny Catechism? Of course I am not. But I am saying that to be a really good novel from a Christian point of view it has got to be such that no one but a Catholic could have written it. (Must I point out that by "Catholic" here I do not

49

mean only those who are explicitly practising members of the
Church? "He that is not against me is for me.")

Am I saying that painters must only paint pictures of starved
Welsh miners? Of course I am not. But I am saying that no painter
can paint a picture without being in effect a propagandist for
something and that, therefore, no decent Catholic painter could
paint a picture whose effect was to add another buttress to the
bourgeois (bourgeois: i.e., buyers and sellers, the founders of
the modern world, in which all things are merchandise, money
is the ruling power and all things are made for the profit of investors).

Of course it's a pity to be too conscious of being a propagandist. It's a pity even in a preacher in the pulpit. But the world's
in a rotten mess and we are the Church Militant (or aren't we?),
so we can't help being a bit more conscious of a mission than if we
were living in a heavenly Jerusalem.

CHAPTER VIII

IT ALL GOES TOGETHER

ACTION is for the sake of contemplation, the active for the sake of the contemplative. To labour is to pray.

Work is the discipline (the yoga) by means of which "body holds its noise and leaves soul free a little."

Recreation is for the sake of work. Leisure time is for the sake of recreation—in order that the labourer may the better return to work. Games are like sleep—necessary for the health of body and mind—a means to health, the health of the workman, the labourer, the man who prays, the contemplative. Leisure is secular, work is sacred. Holidays are the *active* life, the working life is the *contemplative* life.

The object of leisure is work. The object of work is holiness. Holiness means wholeness—it does not mean emaciate or emasculate. The holy man is the complete man—merry because "he nothing lacks"—sad because of the sufferings, failures and penury of others. The holy man is the poor man; having nothing he possesses all things; the Kingdom of Heaven is within him. The spiritual man does not discard or despise the body—he uses the body. The senses are a means to holiness. "Nothing is in the mind but what comes to it through the senses."

It is commonly supposed that in the distinction between "secular and religious" and between "active and contemplative" there is the same distinction as between "work and play," "useful and spiritual," "worldly and otherworldly," "profane and sacred," and so on.

Here are two kinds of misunderstanding, due to (1) failure to distinguish between real words and technical terms (or "jargon"); (2) failure to appreciate the meanings of real words (by "real" words I mean words having a universal signification as distinguished from words having a restricted meaning according to the usage of particular trades and professions).

In ecclesiastical jargon: (1) "Religious" means: according to *rule*. The religious life is the life of those bound by vows to follow a prescribed rule. It does not mean that monks and nuns are more "religious" in the "real" sense than crossing-sweepers or parish priests.

(2) "Secular" means: living in the world; according to the ways and customs of people not bound by "religious" vows. It does not mean that crossing-sweepers and parish priests are more "worldly," less holy, than monks and nuns.

(3) "Active" means: engaged in some work of service to individuals or to society—schools, hospitals, orphanages, the care of the aged or the poor or the outcast—not by way of recreation (as with the Carthusians) but as the object of the rule. (Thus the Sisters of Charity of St. Vincent de Paul are a "religious" organisation, an organisation of "religious" persons bound by a rule with the object of assisting the poor, etc.)

(4) "Contemplative" means: directly engaged in the labour of prayer (personal intercourse with God by means of praise, supplication, meditation—whether discursive or "quiet," etc.) and having no other occupation except for the sake of recreation, or (as commonly with the Benedictines and Cistercians) as a means of livelihood. But in reality the "active" life is also contemplative because to labour is to pray, and the "contemplative" life is also active because to pray is to labour. The distinction in nomenclature is ecclesiastical "jargon."

The purpose of these notes is to draw attention to the confusion and consequent evil caused by our current mixing of jargon and language. We call those activities work in which we engage in order to earn a living. Therefore we associate "active" orders of "religious" men and women with working people, and as the "contemplatives" do not earn their living by doing anything for which they are directly paid, we do not think of them as workers. And as "in the world" when we are not working for our livings we are said to be on holiday, we associate holidays with the life of "contemplation" rather than with the "active life." Thus mooning about, going for a walk on the South Downs, "blue doming," sunbathing (whether at Deauville or in the back garden), swinging in a hammock, hiking and playing golf, we associate with contemplation, and when we finish our holidays and get back to the office or to the study or the factory or the kitchen we say we've got back to work, to activity.

It is not to be denied that it is possible to be more truly "at work" when on holiday than when the holiday is over, nevertheless the general truth remains and properly speaking the holiday is "the active life" and the working life is "the life of contemplation." For, properly speaking, contemplation and work go together and the active life is really the holiday life, the life of recreation. For the holiday life is the animal life, the life of doing, the life in which all things are means—means to health, means to the health which is necessary in order to return to the life of work, the life of prayer, of contemplation, of creation—the life in which God is the immediate end, whereas in the holidays the immediate end is one's own enjoyment, health-giving enjoyment.

The thing to which our present confusion is leading is the thing called *the Leisure State.* We have set up a system of industry, of facture, in which, as its exponents express it, all necessary work shall be done by machinery and thus men will be released for "higher things" in their leisure time. It is the stated aim of the leaders of our world that work shall be reduced to the least possible amount of energy and time and thought.

If they are devout Catholics the ultimate aim of these leaders is that the whole world shall become like a modern Cistercian monastery in which the necessary work, that which is done to provide food, clothing and shelter, shall be regarded as physical recreation. Work in the fields or in the house or workshops shall not be regarded as prayer or contemplation but as a means to these: the choir office, the *opus Dei*. In a modern Cistercian monastery as much as possible of the farm work is done by steam or electrically driven machinery. Such monasteries are dependent upon the modern industrial system to provide them with machines. It is perhaps doubtful whether they will ever be able to make machinery for themselves, and it is perhaps doubtful whether the ironworks and coal-mines, etc., will ever be run on monastic lines. *But that's the bright idea.*

Meanwhile, in order to buy machinery, the monks are dependent either upon large donations from persons who have made large profits in the industrial world or upon the sale of their farm produce at sufficiently profitable rates. For this purpose all or some of the monks must be trained in the ways and methods and mentality of merchants and financiers. And as they do not regard the work of providing food, clothing and shelter as being an *opus Dei,* and itself contemplative, they are able to enter the world of trading with even less scruple than ordinary men—for whom, according to the Christian tradition which prevailed until the industrial revolution, the work of providing physical necessities was holy in itself and the chief means to holiness.

When the leaders of the world are *not* Catholics, their ultimate aim is that the whole world shall become a cultured pleasure park. All necessary work being done by machinery (automatic as much as possible) and in the smallest possible number of hours per year —the labour being either provided voluntarily or by conscription as for national service—the human race will be freed from "the curse of Adam" and will be free to contemplate "the eternal verities" in the long leisure thus secured.

The eternal verities will be such as each individual chooses to think them (though such organisations as the British Broadcasting Corporation and the Board of Education and the Universities will endeavour to lead opinion in the direction favoured by the most cultured persons) and contemplation will vary from the pure "art" of the abstractionists and surrealists to the pure enjoyment of young men and women protected by reliable contraceptives (the police will see to it that the eccentric behaviour of individuals does not disturb the happiness of the greatest number).

It is perhaps doubtful whether such a cultured world will be entirely satisfactory; for men not only desire that the girl shall be charming, and acquiescent if not provocative, but also that the boudoir shall be made to match. The operating-theatre house ("the house is a machine to live in," says the really honest architect of the leisure state) is a beautiful house—as beautiful as a honeycomb or the dissected human eye, as beautiful as standardized, mass-produced motor-cars, and much love-making has been done in such—but it is different in kind from the human beings who live in it, even when the walls are decorated with original paintings by old or modern masters (or by reproductions so like the originals that you wouldn't know the difference), and there are innumerable cushions of the softest make and coloured with all the colours of the aniline spectrum, and there are sculptures by "real artists" and radio Beethoven or dance music—even so, the house, the building itself, the food, the clothing, the funiture— all these things in so far as they are considered *necessary,* will be the product of the admittedly unloved work, got over as soon as possible, of the "Mechanized Necessary Work Corporations" and factories.

Such work, however well and quickly and therefore cheaply done, is of a different kind from (*a*) the love-making of lovers, (*b*) the paintings and sculptures so much prized in museums and on the machine-made walls and (*c*) the food, clothes and furniture of pre-industrial times—times during which, for all their hardships and lack of modern conveniences (sanitation, railways, airplanes, telephones, wireless, motor-cars, tinned food, fountain-pens, typewriters, printing presses working at the rate of 100,000 prints per hour, silk stockings, vacuum cleaners, "Jiffy" washers and God knows what all), food, clothing and furniture as well as houses were all made by human beings with their hands and were often actually and always potentially works of love, of prayer, of contemplation.[1]

It all goes together—industrialism and the leisure state, the potentially contemplative prostituted to the active, the sacred to the profane. Prayer divorced from labour, labour done for the sake of recreation, work for the sake of leisure, leisure for the sake of *self* satisfaction.

[1] When we speak of "pre-industrial times" we do not refer to those times immediately preceding the introduction of factory machinery. We refer to those times before merchants and financiers captured the means of production, distribution and exchange. The coming of machines was indeed a blessed relief from the cruel conditions of the workers in early industrial times.

CHAPTER IX

EATING YOUR CAKE

(Contributed to The Penrose Annual *of 1936)*

I SUPPOSE the saying about "eating your cake and having it" originated in the nursery. Master Tommy ate his cake and then cried to have some. As applied to grown-up affairs it seems to mean the peculiarly British habit of destroying something and then trying to carry on as though the thing still existed. We set up, for example, a great trading enterprise in India, with the natural consequence of placing the native at the mercy of our international finance, and then we talk about "freedom slowly broadening down," or, again, we reduce the power of the king to that of a figure-head (having begun the good work by cutting the head off the figure) and then we go all goofy about jubilees and coronations. We set up a magnificent grid-system of power distribution all over the country and then we become pious about the beauties of rural England. We want it both ways; we want the cake we've eaten.

Notable examples of this foolishness are to be seen in the printing business. To hear our printers and publishers crack on, you would think the "industrial revolution" had never occurred. Architects with their "gothic revivals" and classical façades are foolish enough but, in a literary age, an age in which reading and writing are the compulsory acquirement of every child over five years old and in which books and newspapers are much more numerous than houses, it is truly amazing to see how we refuse to recognize and act upon the consequences of industrial organization.

It is obvious that if we had any sense, if we were the rational beings we think ourselves, we should abolish letters altogether. A collection of signs for sounds which has long since ceased to represent any sounds consistently, and which is in any case a curious collection of odd shapes, would surely have been scrapped long ago by a people having any real enthusiasm for rationality. But assuming that such a reform is not the business of printers or publishers—theirs but to do or die, and so forth—we might suppose that at least they would have taken some trouble to inquire into the rights and wrongs of letter-making and, taking into full account the methods of facture ("manufacture" they still call it, with their passion for quaint turns of speech), they might by now have arrived at a reasonable standard letter. Instead of any such thing, we have a jumble of atrophied remains—vermiform appendixes, adenoids, bald heads, flap-doodle ears and dotty eyes. The reasons are various and obvious. There are the ordinary dull type faces which people can be counted on to endure because they are used to them, the old-styles and newspaper moderns. There are the snob faces, revivals of sixteenth- and eighteenth-century doings, which come to us with all the snob appeal of antique names, Bembo and Fournier and Garamond and Jenson, and then, by way of perverse reaction, there are the Walbaums and Bodonis. I make no mention of the hordes of fancy advertising faces. They are butterflies—they have their life and cease to be—they are means of salesmanship, not to human communication. And all these things exist and nothing else exists simply because printers and publishers, for all their annual-dinner stuff about their "noble craft," are compelled, by the commercial conditions they wallow in and hope to fatten on, to compete with one another for their customers' favour (they call it serving the public) and cannot consider the job of printing as being a job which can be done right or wrong. What's the right way to make a lower-case "a"? "Good

Lord!" they might say, clinging in their habits of speech as in their typography to forms which no longer have any significance, "good Lord! don't ask me, all I know is that Walbaum's very popular at present, though I can't see what's wrong with good old Cheltenham."

But times are changing and the competitive system isn't going on much longer. Whether we go fascist or communist (there's a difference—but that's not the point here) remains to be seen, but there's going to be a "stable price level" one way or another. And then it may again be possible to put the consumer in his place and give him what he ought to have rather than what the poor undisciplined mutt thinks he likes. Let us prepare our minds for that eventuality. All production is for the sake of consumption, but not for the sake of the consumer. We are all consumers anyway, but it is as producers that we know what's what.

Assuming then that we cannot immediately abolish lettering (though I don't see why we shouldn't, considering that with one stroke of the pen a minister of education could make phonography compulsory in every elementary school) let us consider what is a really good alphabet of machine-made letters. It's nothing to do with medieval penmanship. It's very little to do even with what we're used to. It's nothing to do with beauty and good taste as the art-critics use those words. It's a matter of simple rationality, of deciding what is "A" and what is "B," especially what is "a" and what is "b," and so on, bearing in mind the nature of printing surfaces and the technique of machine punch-cutting and type-founding.

Obviously the first thing to do is to cut out or off all unnecessary details, serifs, dots, curly bits, blobs. Having thus arrived at plain letters we can then proceed, by a process of elimination, to discover the most obviously natural or normal forms. Write the letter "a" twenty different times with different proportions of parts. It will be immediately apparent that fifteen or more of your varieties are ridiculous. Try it and see. For one reason (REASON) or another you will then be able to discard four of the remaining five! Do likewise with the whole alphabet. Then consult your pressmen and your type-founders. At the present date this may seem to be no more than a more or less amusing exercise or parlour game. But remember, next year, or sooner, or later, the dictatorship will be upon us. Let's be ready for it. Don't let us have the ridiculous spectacle of Mussolini wearing a collar and tie, Hitler brandishing a toothbrush moustache, Stalin a walrus one and Ataturk wearing a bowler. You can translate these things into typographical terms. We have tried to have a pre-industrial cake in an industrial world; let us not try to preserve our competitive muddle in the non-competitive world.

CHAPTER X

SCULPTURE ON MACHINE-MADE BUILDINGS

A DISCUSSION of the problems of architecture and sculpture to-day necessarily involves us in a consideration of the economic and social, the political and religious background of human life.

No longer can we discuss either architecture or sculpture as academic and isolated subjects concerning architects and sculptors alone.

We are realizing to-day, as perhaps we have not realized in the past, that the work of the world depends upon an almost world-wide co-operation.

It has always been so; but in the presence of a world-wide commercialism the fact is more obvious than it was in times when nations were more self-sufficient and people were fed on the products of their own neighbourhood, clothed with materials grown and woven in their own country and housed in buildings made almost entirely of local materials.

I shall make no apology, therefore, if in this lecture I concern myself more with the economic and social circumstances of the arts than with the particular aesthetic or technical problems which confront architects and sculptors.

Whether we consider that the origin of architectural sculpture (that is to say carving or modelling or statuary on buildings or applied or affixed to them) was the needs or desires of those for

whom the buildings were made, or was the product of the exuberance of the workman, is a problem which does not concern me.

Whichever we decide, it is obvious that the first sculptors were
simply stone masons and carpenters.

There was no distinction between artist and workman. That
distinction is quite a modern one. For the ancients "the artist
was not a special kind of man, but every man was a special kind
of artist."

As the art of building developed the differentiation of trades
developed.

But still the stone carver rose from the ranks of the masons,
and the wood carver from the ranks of the carpenters.

And still they were all workmen together.

This state of things continued (as far as Europe is concerned)
until the fourteenth century and later.

And it still continues in the furniture trade even to-day. The
man who carves furniture does not call himself an artist but a
workman, a wood carver.

And it still continues even in the building trade in those
branches of carving which we call "ornamental," the things architects call "enrichments"—mouldings, capitals of pillars, crockets,
finials.

And in early times the same applied to figure sculpture.

But in the fourteenth century, or thereabouts, a change took
place—gradually.

The medieval conception of life decayed.

The rule of the Church and of princes gave way to the rule
of merchants.

In the sixteenth century (1500 onwards) the merchant class,
which had been subordinate and even despised, gradually emerged
and became the ruling class.

In the early middle ages the money-lender had been generally
despised, even persecuted.

Kings often borrowed from Jews—but they often refused to
pay back.

Usury was not only illegal but execrated.

It was thought not only illegal but wicked.

Bankers were almost unknown in Christendom before the thirteenth century.

Double-entry book-keeping had not been invented.

Manufacture was for use more than for sale.

Markets were only for surplus goods.

International trading was on the smallest scale.

Each country was practically self-supporting.

Imports were only rarities and luxuries—spices and specialties.

Kings and princes were actually rulers.

The man of business, however rich, was more or less despised.

He was not honoured; certainly he was not honoured as such.

He was not a peer of the realm.

The orders of chivalry were not his and he did not aspire to them.

The burgher was a big man in his city, but a small man in the Parliament.

But all things decay and die.

The medieval system was no exception.

The theocratic notion of the state—according to which Revealed religion supplied the principles which guided the rulers and the Church was the superior of the secular power—for the Church answered the questions: "why and wherefore?" and kings and princes were only concerned with "how?"—this theocratic notion was corrupted and eventually dispelled by the rising power of merchants, of traders and bankers.

By the fifteenth century rich merchants were already building churches out of their own money—out of their profits. (As Carnegie and Lord Nuffield build libraries and picture galleries to-day.)

By the sixteenth century they had ceased to build churches and were building themselves country mansions.

The riches of the country were no longer spent on castles and cathedrals, but on private houses and town halls.

And a further development took place:

Money, which during the early middle ages had been usually regarded as something to spend, a thing giving powers to its possessor over the labour of others and not a thing which could itself be bought and sold—now became a thing to save for investment.

It was discovered that you could get round the Christian laws against usury by calling money-lending "investment" and by calling the interest "a share in the profits."

Hitherto the borrower had been regarded as a poor man in difficulties and it had been considered sinful to take advantage of his difficulties by charging him interest.

But now the borrower was not so much the man in difficulties as "the man of enterprise" who held out to the lender opportunities of enrichment.

And the lender was not so much a kindly helpful person, or a wicked usurer, as a person who saw a chance of increasing his wealth by financing your enterprise.

This is not a history of commercialism. It is sufficient to point out that the rise to supremacy of the financier—a supremacy which we have seen completed in our own times—was necessarily accompanied by the degradation of the small trader and the small craftsman.

And it was accompanied by a degradation of the whole idea of labour and craftsmanship.

The workman everywhere became the employee.

He became the irresponsible "hand" in a factory, owning nothing but his labour power, a proletarian dependent for his very existence upon the wages reluctantly meted out to him—wages which, in the absence of trades unions, were naturally kept down to the lowest level consistent with keeping him alive.

The whole idea of commerce, as run by our men of business, since the breakdown of medieval theocracy, is the reduction of the costs of production and the increase of profits.

To buy cheap and sell dear.

To pay as little as possible to labourers and charge as much as possible to consumers.

Gradually this idea of things came to prevail everywhere and among all classes.

Both the aristocracy and the labourers were corrupted by it.

Under its influence and dazed by the material aggrandisement which the wealth of merchants produced, it seemed, even to the landed gentry, that no other motive than desire of gain could be expected to rule in human hearts.

This was not altogether surprising in the case of the gentry, for they themselves, in the majority of cases, owed their wealth to the spoliation of the monastic and ecclesiastical possessions at the Reformation.

And it was not surprising in the case of the labourers, for in the course of several generations they forgot their traditions and could imagine no other kind of life than that of servile instruments in the hands of avaricious employers.

Thus it came about that the theocratic idea of human society everywhere gave place to the commercial idea and the economic interpretation of history came to be regarded as the only valid one.

And when, goaded by the spur of their insupportable burdens, the labourers were able, at long last and after much bloodshed and cruelty, to force trades unionism upon the masters, this economic interpretation of history was taken for granted by the unions and no attempt was made to regain the responsibility of the medieval guilds.

The modern trade unionist takes it for granted that the lot of the employee is simply that of a "hand," an obedient tool, a sentient part of the machinery. It does not occur to him that things were ever otherwise, or that it could ever be possible that he could *own* his work, still less that he could ever have any intellectual responsibility for its *form or quality*.

Moreover, the division and subdivision of labour which was necessary for the profit of his master could have no other effect

than to make him as intellectually irresponsible as his proletarianism had made him economically impotent.

Perhaps it will not be at first sight obvious what all this has
to do with architecture and sculpture.

But art is not an abstraction.

It is the actual works of men—the things they make, and the
things they make are the things they like and want.

In any survey of human works we have to consider what kind
of men were paramount in their production.

In considering architecture and sculpture to-day we must consider the influences bringing them into being and moulding their
existence.

And no survey of architecture and sculpture can neglect their
historical circumstances.

And historical circumstances include the rise and fall of governors.

He who pays the piper calls the tune.

That is the fact that all art critics and historians of the arts
forget or neglect.

They talk and write as though artists (including in that word
architects and painters and sculptors and musicians and poets)
were a sort of aristocracy or even dictatorship who produce whatever they fancy and force it upon a world of sycophants who can
do nothing but gratefully accept what they are given.

This is far from the truth.

It is a superstition which it pays certain people to foster, but
which only resembles the truth in a few rare cases.

It is only true in those rare cases in which the artist, like a
religious ascetic, is prepared to starve rather than do anything but
what seems to him the will of God as directly revealed to him
individually.

But the work of the world is not done like that.

The work of the world is done in response to *demand*. The
modern breakdown of demand has made necessary modern salesmanship—the "breaking down of sales resistance."

Men want things and are prepared to pay for them.

Workmen are trained to make things and obtain a living by selling them—

That is by exchanging what they make for bread and butter and clothes and houses.

The baker exchanges bread for clothes and houses.

The builder exchanges buildings for clothes and bread.

And the clothier exchanges coats and trousers for bread and buildings.

And there is no special person called an artist who holds a spiritual pistol to our heads, saying:

Give me bread and clothes and houses and I will give you— what it suits my high and lofty mind to give.

For, in spite of the cackle of art critics and dealers, the painter of pictures and the sculptor and the architect and the musician and the poet cannot sell their goods unless someone will buy them.

And people won't buy what they do not want.

Although, for a time, by skilful flattery and advertisement you can persuade people to buy things just to be in the fashion.

Gas cookers are fashionable one year—electric the next.

Sham Gothic was fashionable in 1 8 3 0, sham "modern" in 1 9 3 0, and so on.

But however it be done—whether by flattery or fraud or honest trading—the man who makes things must be paid.

And people won't pay unless they want his goods.

And so, in a general way, what people make is what they think people want.

It is urgently important to bear these primary facts in mind when we consider such matters as architecture and sculpture.

Otherwise we shall be wandering in an unreal world—the world of art critics—and we shall talk and theorize as though styles of building and styles of sculpture had no relation to the ideas and ideals of the people who pay for them.

In thus insisting on the necessity of taking into account the ideas of the client or customer or buyer I am not suggesting that we should all embrace the philosophy of materialism according to which the economic interpretation of history is the only true one.

For though I maintain that the ideas and enthusiasms of the artist, the workman, are conditioned by those of his customer just as the ideas of the customer are conditioned by those of the artist, I am not therefore saying the economic circumstances are the *ruling* circumstances in either case.

Because I cannot always be making what I am never able to sell and because my customer will not, in a general way, pay money for what he does not like or need, it does not follow that either of us is concerned chiefly with the money or economic aspect of the work.

It does not follow that either of us will sacrifice *everything* for money.

There is fair give and take.

The relationship in a normal society is one of reciprocity.

The point is precisely that.

I do not make merely what pleases my fancy, not giving a damn what anybody says.

The customer cannot, *in a normal society,* coerce the workman.

Neither is a mere worm to be trodden by the other.

And neither is a tyrant.

Now the point of all these remarks on the relation between workman and customer is to draw attention to the fact that the styles of building and the styles of sculpture must always be thought of as representing the time in which they were produced in all its aspects and not merely in what I may call its "studio" aspect, though that is the aspect which alone interests the art critic.

When we observe the change in the style of architecture which occurred in the fifteenth and sixteenth centuries, we have to consider this change not as being simply due to a change in the ideas of architects but as being as much due to a change in the ideas,

68

ideals, ways of life and ways of thinking of the people for whom they worked.

Styles of art are always consonant with and representative of styles of thinking and the thinking is not only done by the artist —for the man he works for has got to pay for it and he won't pay money for what he can't live with—things which don't suit his way of living.

Moreover, the artist himself is not precisely a God. He does not create out of nothing. His mind has to be fed, and those who feed it are to a very large extent those who pay for what he makes.

And the outstanding thing to notice about the change which occurred in the fifteenth and sixteenth centuries is that it was precisely the kind of change which, if you'd been clever enough to think of it, was the very one best calculated to tickle the fancy of the newly enfranchised, growing, and growing more and more powerful, class of rich merchants and bankers.

The Medicis, the Fuggers, like their modern counterparts the Rothschilds and Harmsworths and Sassoons and Leverhulmes and Nuffields, quite naturally and inevitably fell for a revival of the splendours of decadent Rome and the slave culture of the pre-Christian world.

Were they not themselves the founders of a new slavery?

Naturally they admired everything which smelt of the old one.

While scholars and antiquarians rummaged about in the Graeco-Roman ruins and waxed enthusiastic about the remains of Nero and Caligula, Cicero and Horace, these founders of our commercialism were perfecting their account-keeping and their system of money lending—

They were also lining their pockets.

And what more suitable than that they should build imitation Roman palaces and pay painters to paint their portraits and the portraits of their expensive women?

From their point of view nothing was so admirable, nothing so well worth painting as portraits of themselves and their ladies. And, apart from portraits, nothing was so delightful as pictures of heathen mythology and the loves and sports of heathen gods.

These things gave them no qualms.

They expressed no criticism.

They laid no burdens on their consciences.

What Diana did, or Apollo, had no reference to their money-makings, their successful dealings in money and merchandise, their slave raids into Africa and the newly discovered Americas.

They could pursue these affairs and suffer no rebuke.

Even the Churches they built—for they still built Churches and they still gave lip worship to the God of the Christians—after all the clergy are quite useful as agents for keeping the rank and file of the workers in order—a licentious upper class is more or less manageable, but a licentious labouring class is very unprofit-able—and it will always be a true saying: *religio instrumentum regni* (religion is the instrument of the ruler), as they still agree in Fascist Italy—

I say even the Churches they built were decorated with imita-tion Graeco-Roman ornamentation—cherubs and nymphs and acanthus leafage, and even the Christian Saints were forced to posture in attitudes derived from the Roman bacchanalia.

The civilization of the Middle Ages had broken down by rea-son of its own internal corruptions.

But they themselves, the money-lenders and merchants, were themselves the engines of that corruption.

They were the actual germ of the disease.

The whole idea of the Christian economy as it emerged from the peace of Constantine, or at least its spear head, had been the subordination of commerce and the suppression of usury. The worship of riches was everywhere condemned.

A multitude of "religious" men and women flourished under the banner of poverty, chastity and obedience.

A whole cohort of saints were honoured at Christian altars whose chief claim to honour was their renunciation of riches, their humility, their self-sacrifice.

We think all this worship very foolish and old-fashioned.

In the Middle Ages such people were the people they vener-
ated.

And as long as money-making and business chicanery was rep-
robated and usury punished, so long the medieval culture grew
and flowered.

But all things pass.

The merchant was not to be for ever subordinated.

He brings gifts not to be for ever despised.

The gradual enslavement of the poor seemed, even to moral-
ists and philosophers, not too high a price to pay for a higher
standard of life—and that is the point of view to-day of the poor
themselves. Security and comfort are better than responsibility.

But the point here is not political or religious.

The thing I am trying to elucidate is the fact that the movement we call the Renaissance was not merely or even chiefly a
movement of artists and men of learning acting independently
of men of affairs—men of business and politicians.

The Renaissance, as an artistic affair, was simply the visible
flowering and expression of the triumph of the mercantile class
at the end of the Middle Ages.

The world had returned to slavery—it was right and proper
and natural and understandable that it should return to the worship of a slave architecture.

And, even more important, it was natural that it should return
to self-worship and the worship of humanity—to nature worship
and naturalistic painting and sculpture—to all those things which
characterize the culture of successful trading nations.

For the accurate imitation of natural appearance, the accurate
representation of human anatomy and perspective and the light
and shade of landscape upon which so much energy and study has
been expended during the last four centuries, are quite naturally
the sort of things which seem important to the rather low-class
minds of the merchant and trading classes—the successful and
ruling classes of our era.

For though what a thing means or signifies is obviously more important than what a thing looks like or reminds you of—to shopkeepers and bankers the meaning of things is altogether too difficult to be grasped.

Moreover meanings are often unflattering.

The Gospel story and the dogmas of religion are almost wholly inimical to the ideas of commerce—

"How hardly shall a rich man enter into the Kingdom of Heaven!"

"Woe to you, rich men! Weep in your miseries which shall come upon you—Your riches are putrid."

"Blessed are the poor in spirit. . . ."

"Take no thought for the morrow"—insurance, dividends, profits, next year's wheat harvest, "futures."

"Be not solicitous. . . ."

"Seek first the Kingdom of God and his justice. . . ."

Such sayings must naturally be unpopular among men whose whole life is one long flouting of them.

And works of painting and sculpture done in illustration of the doctrines of Christianity must naturally be less popular among lord-mayors and bankers than more or less meaningless representations of nymphs and goddesses, especialy if the said nymphs and goddesses are shown more or less naked.

And if there must still be churches and church paintings and sculptures—at least let them be "life-like."

Let them be good imitations of the things we love.

Let the angels be pretty.

Let the figure of Christ look as harmless as a hair-dresser.

Under such auspices it was only to be expected that the development of painting and sculpture should follow the same lines as they had followed in ancient Greece and Rome in similar circumstances.

Just as Greek sculpture had proceeded from its early beginnings as the servant of high religion to its end as the pander and flatterer of successful politicians and usurers—and, in the process, from a lovely but austere and hieratic iconography to a simpering and sentimental idealization of visual appearance.

So the hieratic art of the religion-dominated Middle Ages proceeded from its simple beginnings in the early Byzantine and Romanesque and Saxon and Celtic, through the fine flowering of the eleventh and twelfth centuries to its inevitable decay in the mechanically expert but spiritually empty works of the flamboyant and ornate age of the Tudors.

And this progress corresponded at every point with the growth of commerce and the increasing dominance of merchants and their masters the bankers and usurers.

Look at any church or town hall of the fifteenth century— in England, France or Germany—observe how the masons and carvers have succumbed to a mere lust for ostentation; observe the endless repetition of heraldic snobberies, the elaboration of vaulting and wall panellings.

Ask yourselves if people in such a state of mind would not take, like ducks to water, to the resuscitation of Graeco-Roman splendour.

It was exactly the jam they wanted.

And with such people for customers, naturally an impetus would be given to naturalistic painting and sculpture.

They could understand and appreciate that sort of thing.

Just as to-day, the one thing the ordinary man of business appreciates (and are not the vast majority of our fellow-countrymen men of business and imbued with the commercial mentality)— the one thing he appreciates is that which he can easily recognize as being a likeness of something he likes—a view of the place where he spent his summer holiday or a "speaking likeness" of himself or his wife or daughters.

Let us not be side-tracked by the high art criticism of the art critics.

Their stuff is all right in its own line.

Painters and sculptors in their studios are aflame with aesthetic enthusiasms and despise the anecdotage of their customers.

Schools rise and fall.

One aestheticism gives place to another and in the select cote-
ries of the connoisseurs pure abstraction is the present fashion—
unless surrealism has just taken its place.

But we need not consider these things—this studio business.

What we are concerned with is architecture and architectural
sculpture and these things are more important than what goes on
in studios and picture galleries—because buildings are still, and
always must be, things which everybody uses and sees. They can
never be the *objets d'art* which art dealers deal in.

They can only very rarely be bought by American millionaires
and put in museums.

Nevertheless, what I have said about the tastes of men of business in the matter of paintings and sculptures, applies very obviously to buildings.

The architecture of Greece and Rome is naturally sympathetic
to him.

It has just that pompousness which pleases him and gives his
customers the right feeling of his financial stability.

And above all it is a slave architecture.

Greece and Rome were slave civilizations.

The rank and file of Greek and Roman labourers were mere
"hands" just as modern workmen are.

And so, during the whole period from the fifteenth century to
the beginning of the nineteenth, from the end of the Middle Ages
to the "industrial revolution," from the end of the guilds to the
coming of the machine, it was right and proper that architectural
magnificence, whether domestic, civil or ecclesiastical, should be
modelled on that of Rome.

It was more and more a slave architecture, just as our civilization became more and more a slave civilization.

The early exuberances and funny business of the Tudor and
Jacobean dynasties gave place to the solid classicism of Queen
Anne and the Georges. Whitehall, Chelsea Hospital, Chatsworth,
Birmingham Town Hall—the Four Courts.

A steady procession from funny to dull and from dull to duller—ending up with such things as Buckingham Palace and Selfridge's.

But the real sham classic business ended in the 1790's.

The machine killed it.

The inhuman killed the subhuman.

Up to the industrial revolution, as in Greece and Rome, however servile the condition of the labourer, he was at any rate a human being.

And in the absence of miles of cheap drawing paper, architects, much against their wills no doubt, had to rely on the workmen as being possessed of a considerable deal of knowledge, initiative, sensibility and responsibility.

You had to leave a certain amount of responsibility to the workman simply because you couldn't draw out everything on paper.

You couldn't draw everything simply because there wasn't paper enough.

Rolls of "detail paper" didn't exist!

There was, therefore, a certain liveliness, a certain humanity in building even after three centuries of an increasingly commercial commercialism.

And though the R.A. kind of artist was becoming grander and grander and the gulf between the ordinary architectural carver and the West End studio sculptor was becoming deeper and wider, it was still true to say that the common stone-carver was the same kind of being as the academician, and the man who carved the acanthus leaves was the same kind of being as the common mason.

Everything went together, if only for the simple reason that everything was made by hand and all workmen were responsible for what they made.

But though in its methods of workmanship architecture remained human up to the end of the eighteenth century, there is one respect in which slave architectures differ from the architectures of free men which architects had not realized.

In slave architectures sculpture is an extra ordered by the architect and placed as he chooses. It is not a product of the exuberance of the workman. It does not grow from the walls of building but from the commands of the architect.

It does not in any way spring from the fact that the workman is a member of the building gang and a sharer in the ideas, enthusiasms and wishes of those who will actually use the building. The workman does not count.

The building is not in any sense *his* building.

He is neither responsible for any part of its design nor does he expect to use the building as his own.

The devitalizing effect of this state of affairs is not obvious as long as the old, hand methods of workmanship continued.

In spite of the omnipotence of the architect, the actual workman remained a responsible agent and collaborator.

If the architect decreed mouldings or carvings, the job of doing the said mouldings or carvings was still a job requiring the responsible artistic collaboration of the mason and stone-carver.

And precisely the same tools and technique were employed by carvers as by masons. Both worked in the same workshops or on the job itself.

Even the bricklayer was a responsible craftsman, like the mason or carpenter, and brickmaking itself, however simple and almost mechanical in its technique, was still a job in which each individual brick required the responsible determination of the brickmaker to make it.

Exactly as the sculptor must use his imagination in order to see in his mind's eye the final shape of his sculpture, so, simple though it was, the brickmaker had to have, in his mind, the idea of the brick to be made before he made it.

The difference between one workman and another, however widely separated in skill or worldly esteem, was a difference of degree, not of kind.

Therefore if the architect decreed carvings on his building, he was not decreeing something different in its physical or mental or technical origins from the rest of the work to be done.

The mason and the bricklayer were in fact a kind of sculptors —sculptors were a kind of masons.

In these circumstances, though architecture reflected more and more closely the mercantile ambitions, snobberies and luxuries of the period, it still remained a human art, an *humane* art.

For though devices for saving or displacing labour, such as wind-mills and water-mills, had been in use for centuries and various elementary forms of steam-engines for pumping were invented and were in use long before 1750, the most important development had been the creation of a proletariat.

By the systematic dispossession of the peasantry, by means of the enclosure of common lands and the amalgamations of small farms, it had been possible, so it was claimed, greatly to increase the agricultural production, yet, at the same time, a landless labouring class had been created.

This fitted in very well with the growth of manufacture. The supply of cheap labour was multiplied.

Landless men flocked with their families into the towns.

The towns grew and the system of factory organization grew also.

Long before there was anything that we can properly call "machine production" there was division and subdivision of hand labour.

In fact it is true to say that the first stage of machine production was the conversion of the human beings themselves into machines.

The *human* machine preceded the machine made of metal.

The machine worked by blood and muscle preceded the machine worked by steam.

In the early factories things were machine-made, but the machines employed were human beings—men, women and children.

It was but a short and easy step under the spur of commercial

competition and avarice, and in a country like England, well
supplied with iron and coal easily accessible and easily obtained
and with a hungry proletariat clamouring for work and not in a
position to refuse to work under any conditions, however cruel—
it was a short and easy step from production by hand to machine
production properly so-called.

One invention led to another. The foreign market for cheap
factory articles seemed insatiable. The home market was of course
negligible, for the wages of factory hands were kept as low as
possible—trade unionism was repressed if not prohibited—and
foreign nations with an even lower "standard of living" had not
yet entered into the competition.

By the middle of the nineteenth century the original idea of
machinery—that it was a means of *power* and power only, had
given way to the idea of machinery as a substitute for *skill*.

The old machines *did* things—turned mill wheels, pumped
water, ground corn, pulled coal trucks and passenger trains.

Gradually machines were invented not merely to do, but to
make.

Little by little the responsibility of the workman was reduced.

He became less and less a maker, more and more a machine-
minder.

He had been, in the majority of trades, a less and less responsible workman even before the advent of modern machinery.

He had been reduced to being a kind of machine himself.

Now he was less even than that.

His responsibility as a maker was taken away from him entirely. Henceforth the machine does the making; the workman
is only a chauffeur—a person who feeds and drives and tends the
machine.

He was reduced, as the theologian puts it, to "a sub-human
condition of intellectual irresponsibility."

Great numbers of such men are, of course, skilled mechanics
and highly responsible workmen. But there is one thing they are
not responsible for, are not expected to be and have lost all wish

to be, and that is *the form and quality* of the things which the machine makes!

Apart from their interest in the machines themselves, the workers of to-day cannot be said to be interested in their work at all.

And those who are really interested in the machines are only a small proportion of the workers; for the majority are not even responsible mechanics, but are concerned simply to perform some simple routine and almost automatic operation and are interested only in what they are going to do when they are not working.

I am not at all saying that factory hands don't like being factory hands—there's plenty of evidence to the contrary, and "enlightened self-interest" has made it plain that good business depends much more on the health and happiness of the "hands" than the early factory owners had any reason to think.

I am only concerned with the fact that modern machine-made things are of a different *kind* from what existed before machinery and with the consequent fact that what we call "industrial design," though it is still concerned with the design of things *for* human beings, is no longer concerned with the design of things made *by* human beings.

Now all this business of machinery and machine production applies to the building trade as much as to furniture and utensils and clothes and motor-cars.

And it is only the extremely "die-hard" traditions of pre-industrial building and manufacture which prevent us from realizing the fundamental change which has taken place in human works.

It is natural enough that those traditions should take a lot of killing. How many centuries have gone to their building up!

If it is difficult, well-nigh impossible, to get tailors to leave out the buttons on the back of a frock coat—although they are hardly visible and of no use whatever—how much more difficult is it to get furniture makers to leave out the carving and ornament when you consider that such carving and ornament are very much looked at and not only help to sell the stuff but also have the great advantage of covering up bad material and bad construction.

And how much more difficult for architects to leave out mouldings and pillars and sculptures!

It is not exactly that these things help to sell the building (though even that is not wholly true) nor do they hide bad construction, though they do distract attention from feebleness of design.

The difficulty here is twofold:

1. In the first place, during the course of centuries, and especially the last four centuries, a tremendous solemnity has surrounded the whole business of architectural ornament.

When people go to look at old cathedrals or the ruins of classical temples, the sculptures and carvings are, I regret to say, the things that seem to impress them most.

And when you think of such things as the Elgin marbles you are at once in an atmosphere of almost magical solemnity and architects cluck about the sculptures of the Parthenon almost as though the building were the hen and the sculptures the precious egg which she had laid.

It is almost as though architects *dared* not leave out the sculptures.

And then think of the books about it! The dictionaries of ornament—classic and Gothic. . . .

2. And in the second place there is the client!

Even though the architect preferred to do plain building he would still have the client to contend with.

For though few clients care about sculpture or painting in themselves, they care a good deal, and quite naturally and legitimately, what the building they are paying for looks like from the street.

From their point of view a building is not only a place to work in or conduct business in but is also an advertisement.

Grand, swagger buildings with expensive-looking carving on them give an impression of "big business" and importance.

Just as the prosperous merchant flaunts his gold watch-chain, so he wants his offices to flaunt sculptures and pediments.

And the same thing applies to private houses.

The bit of "stained glass" in the front door was put there quite as much to impress visitors and neighbours as because the builder cared about it. And the same applies to all the other ornamental extras.

Snobbery and display in a commercial world account for architectural magnificence much more than the wishes of architects or the exuberance of workmen—

Indeed, the exuberance of workmen has long since ceased to exist.

But just as "all good things come to an end," so do all bad things. And as the application of hand-made sculptures to machine-made buildings is now seen by most architects (or at least by most of the young ones) to be an absurdity—as absurd as applying hand-made wrought ironwork to the Forth Bridge—
as absurd as hand-painted decorations on a motor-car bonnet—
as absurd as tassels on a telephone instrument—
so the use of ornament, sculptured or painted, and architectural enrichment for the sake of social or business ostentation and advertisement is seen to be both ridiculous and disgusting—as ridiculous and as disgusting as the use of carving on furniture to hide the bad materials and bad construction.

Therefore, both from the technical and the social points of view, we are led to the conclusion that architectural sculpture has no place in modern building.

Neither the good architect nor the decent client want it.

There is, however, another and more positive line of argument.

What, after all, *is* architecture?

Is it not obvious that a building, as such, is a thing having its own rights to existence? ·

Architecture is *building*; it is *construction*.

It should be obvious that it is possible to look at a building and to judge it good or bad quite apart from any reference to ornament or sculptures.

Look, for instance, at any of the Norman castles which still remain, ruined or unruined.

What architect, or even what tourist, will complain because they are not sculptured like the north porch of Chartres?

When you look at the remains of the temples at Paestum, does it even occur to you that they are devoid of sculpture?

I have already referred to the Forth Bridge. There is a noble work of architecture! Is it the worse for being devoid of ornament?

If then it is clear, as it is clear, that we have developed a system of industry which has reduced the individual workman to the position of an irresponsible tool—
and if it is clear, as it is clear, that commercial and social swank and aggrandisement are not proper motives for the application of architectural ornament and sculptures to buildings which are of their own nature not productive of such—it should be equally clear that architects should give up all those outworn and threadbare conventions which were the product of a quite different age and a quite different system of industry, and there need be no tears shed—least of all by architects.

Speaking in the abstract a man may say he would rather fly than walk.

But when you are skating on ice, you do not complain because the technique of skating does not readily allow of leapfrog. There is a special quality and delightfulness about skating which is a sufficing joy in itself.

So though, in the abstract, you may say the Cathedral of Chartres is more completely beautiful than the Forth Bridge, nevertheless in our industrial and mechanical age we are not only fools to build imitation Gothic churches, but we are even bigger fools *not* to build the specially fine buildings which such an age is specially equipped to build.

To cry over spilt milk is foolish enough; but not to drink the milk we have is more foolish by far.

In a lecture addressed to architects there is perhaps no need to say anything about sculptors. Many are now out of work and many more will be out of work in the near future.

But there is this further to be said *to architects,* and it may perhaps be comforting to sculptors:—

There is a kind of sculpture which, though not strictly speaking architectural, is nevertheless intimately connected with architecture and destined to be wanted in the future as much as in the past.

This is the sculpture of images which are required, not by the architect as an embellishment to his building (though they may accidentally embellish it and should do so), but which are required by the owner or user of the building as signifying its use or purpose.

The most obvious example of this kind of sculpture is a crucifix on a Catholic church.

A crucifix on a church is not put there because the architect thinks it would be pretty, or because it would perhaps mark "a focus point" in his composition, but *simply and solely* because the owners and users of the building require it.

There are many such occasions for sculpture and it would be all to the good of sculpture itself if sculptors were to regard themselves as performing a service in that way and would forget their high aesthetic entanglements.

And it would be all to the good of both architecture and sculpture if architects would forget all about sculpture as ornament and enrichment and would only use it where it was a real necessity insisted upon by the client.

Only let architects and sculptors and painters remember that there are from a proper point of view no such things as *decorative* sculpture or painting, and that there are no such things as *symbolic* sculpture or painting.

Things are required or not required—necessary or unnecessary.

And sculptures and paintings are themselves things and not pictures of things.

A symbol is a thing which signifies something else.

But first of all it is a thing itself.

Thus the *Union Jack* symbolizes Great Britain (and part of Ireland).

But first of all it is itself a real thing. It is a real piece of cloth with real crosses on it.

And the man who makes it has to be a real weaver and know exactly how to make crosses.

And only because the flag is really there, real cloth and real crosses, is it capable of being a symbol.

Anything can be used as a symbol—any *thing,* but it must first of all be a thing.

From a sculptor's point of view, what a thing is is more important than what his customer uses it to symbolize.

Thus we say a figure of *Cupid* symbolizes love.

But that was not how the first Greek sculptors thought about it.

For them a figure of Cupid was an image of a God—The God of Love, Love incarnate.

The sculptor's job was not symbolism, but portraiture.

He had to make an image as like the God as possible.

If he worked in stone, his job was not to make stone look like flesh and blood, but to make a stony version of a real person, a person he really believed in, and just because he was working in stone, and not in flesh and blood, he had to concentrate on the real nature of the God and not upon the merely transient accidents of flesh. He had to use his imagination more than his eyes. He had to imagine what the God really was, rather than copy his merely flesh and blood appearance. He had first of all to *believe* in the God, he had to believe in order to see. Instead of saying "seeing is believing," he said: to believe is to see.

84

It was only when the reality of the God ceased to be believed in that Greek sculpture went to rot—as it did in Athens.

And that is why Victorian "symbolic sculpture" is all such b. nonsense—because the very idea of it is nonsense. It is all seeing and no believing.

The whole Renaissance idea of painting and sculpture (like that of decadent Greece and Rome) is based upon seeing.

They set up models.

They teach anatomy.

They study the appearance of nature.

What things *are* does not interest them, they are only concerned with how things *look*.

And this idea pervades the whole world.

So that even believers are corrupted by it.

So that even devout Christians or Hindus, when they have been trained in art schools, only succeed in producing things suitable for the boudoirs of the bourgeois.

It is the same with all symbols and symbolic things.

Lettering for example—the letter A symbolizes certain sounds in language.

But the letter cutter's business is not symbolism but letter cutting.

The letter A is a thing made in a certain way.

To discover that way is the letter cutter's first concern.

Victorian furniture, for example—a Victorian drawing-room symbolizes the whole Victorian period—its virtues and vices, its material prosperity and its spiritual bankruptcy—but Messrs. Maple & Co. were not "symbolic artists"—they made tables and chairs as they thought tables and chairs ought to be made, and in the most profitable manner.

Photography, for example—a photograph of your sweetheart symbolizes "young English girlhood," shall we say? But the photographer's job is not symbolism, but photography.

And it is the same with all pictures.

85

The painter's job is painting—making in paint the thing his customer wants and in a way suitable to the stuff called paint.

("What I ask of a painting," says Maurice Denis, "is that it shall look like paint.")

And in the same way there should be, from the sculptor's point of view, no such things as "ornaments" or "decorative" sculptures in the modern senses of those words.

To wear a crown is to wear something necessary or appropriate to the nature or function of the wearer.

A crown is not an ornament or decoration except in the strict sense—as when they say on dinner invitations "decorations will be worn," and as in church rubrics they refer to the crucifix and candles as "ornaments" of the altar—i.e., necessary and appropriate *furniture*.

The whole business of ornament and decoration as understood by architects is false. It is a product of the slave cultures of decadent Greece and Rome.

A crucifix, for instance, is not an ornament except in the sense just mentioned; it is either necessary or unnecessary.

And a crucifix is not a picture of Christ on the cross; it *is* Christ on the cross—Christ himself in wood or stone, as Christ himself would be if he were *made* of wood or stone—a wooden Christ or a stone Christ, not an imitation in wood or stone of a Christ made of flesh and blood.

And flowers and leaves and figures and patterns painted or carved on walls or pillars are either necesary or unnecessary.

If there are no reasons but outworn convention and ostentation for doing them, they should be omitted. Such work degrades both doer and beholder.

We must be "born again" in this as in other matters.

In conclusion I will point out that my main object in this lecture has been to draw attention to the actually existing conditions of building.

For though we take it for granted that the workman on the scaffold does not count at all, has no say in the matter, has no right to any say and no power or ability to make any say, yet we are entirely oblivious of the fact that to a very large extent we are still designing buildings in styles of architecture which belong to and developed in pre-industrial times—times in which the workman on the scaffold not only had a say in the work he did, but was competent to say it.

We have, in effect, abolished the human workman (except as a loyal and efficient tool or hand) and yet we still design buildings as though the human workman was still the builder.

The conclusion is obvious:

Either we must abandon our industrialism, and return to humane methods of working and building, or *we must build industrial buildings*—that is to say: buildings of a kind and in a style suitable to the industrial, commercial, mechanical age of which the majority of us is so proud.

You cannot have it both ways.

You cannot gather figs of thistles.

You cannot improve machine-made buildings by the addition of hand-made sculptures.

CHAPTER XI

ART IN ENGLAND NOW . . .
AS IT SEEMS TO ME

*A broadcast talk given at Jerusalem 15 June 1937; with
additions*

LADIES AND GENTLEMEN: Please do not be put off on account of
the title of this talk. I am not going to speak about the mysteries
of aesthetics. Strange as it may seem, art is simply the business of
making things—anything and everything.

Art is not just the so-called "fine arts"—painting pictures, making statues, writing poetry or musical symphonies.

For there is also the art of the dentist and that of the mason;
the art of the cook, and the art of the printer . . .

There is also the art of architecture and building and this art
combines all others: masonry, painting, wood-working and glass
and engineering.

For there is also the art of the engineer! Engineering is simply
architecture (building, construction) denuded of everything that
is not capable of being measured. Engineering is mathematical
architecture.

So art is the whole business of human making and there is no
hard and fast line between "art" and "fine art." For if we say the
fine arts are the arts of making things which please us by their
beauty, and that the other arts are simply the arts of making what
is useful, we only confuse ourselves—because there is no reason

why useful things should not please us by their beauty and there is no reason why pictures and statues and poems and songs should be considered useless.

After all we don't put statues in public squares just to look nice. They are put there for the useful, the quite *useful* purpose of teaching us, as the poet says, that "we can make *our* lives sublime"—think of all our political heroes! There's sublimity. . . .

And we don't put pictures of saints in church windows just to look pretty—or do we?

And portrait painting is supposed to be "fine art"—but the portrait of the King on a postage stamp or a coin is not put there to be beautiful but to do a useful job—like a signature on a cheque.

.   .   .   .   .

And, on the other hand, chairs and tables and pots and pans are not simply useful.

In order to be suitable for human use they have to be good to look at also.

What about clothes for example?

Are clothes nothing to us but useful protections against the weather or against prying eyes?

You know it is not so.

Clothes are for dignity and adornment quite as much as and perhaps much more than for warmth or modesty.

.   .   .   .   .

In brief, it is best simply to say that "art is making well what is wanted" and the beautiful is "that which being seen pleases"; for all well-made things are pleasing *to our minds*—whether pictures or pots—pleasing to our *minds*.

But there's no reason why we shouldn't train our minds a bit.

.   .   .   .   .

Well . . . art in England . . . as it seems to me!

England! England? What is England? England is the reputed centre of world finance, world trade, world money-making. London, New York, Paris, Berlin—but remember London began the modern international industrialism. We must never forget this when we talk or think about art! Money, in our world, is the first, the ruling consideration.

The rest is either camouflage—or frills and furbelows.

What about art in England, then?

On the one hand there is the factory system—the industrial system. On the other hand there are the artists' studios! Remember—art is *all* making—not just paintings and such.

First let us briefly consider the *factory system*—industrialism. The factory system is the system by which things are produced as much as possible by machinery and as much as possible in mass—mass production. Thus the cost of production is reduced. And in this system the labour of men is regarded simply as a "cost." Therefore, labour must be reduced as much as possible. Hence "labour-saving" machinery, and, in the up-to-date modern factory, the labourer is not so much a man as a part of the machinery. They use men and women only for jobs they have not yet invented machines to do.

So the ordinary workman has been reduced to a sub-human condition of intellectual irresponsibility—as the theologian puts it.

The only responsible factory workmen are the gangers and overseers. And the only persons responsible for the form and quality of what the machines turn out are the designers of the machines. The rest are just "hands"—instruments. They are only fully human when they are not working—if then.

The system is only really suitable for the production of plain necessities—plain drain pipes, telephone wires, matches.

For when the method of production is completely mechanical, then if we were wise, we should use it only for the production of purely mechanical things. Because machines don't "do" ornament, it's not in their nature. Dignity and adornment! What's that got to do with machines and money-making?

But ordinary human beings won't have things plain, because they are human and not mechanical beings.

So, as machinery is used for everything, including ornamental things, they have to employ designers to add ornament and so give a saleable quality to the products.

So the main part of the ordinary things used by men and women—food, clothing, furniture, pots and pans and building materials—are made by machinery.

On the other hand, people still want pictures and sculptures and so a special class of people called "artists" has come into existence.

These special people are quite cut off from the ordinary needs of life

and so they become very eccentric and more and more peculiar

and their works become more and more expensive

and so they are bought only by very rich people

and so artists have become like hot-house flowers, or lap-dogs

and so their works are more and more as peculiar as themselves

and so we have all the new kinds of "art movements"

and so what we call Art (with a largeA) is now simply a sort of psychological self-exhibitionism.

They say art is "self-expression"—they say so themselves.

Before modern machine industrialism, art used to be the expression of the mind of the whole people. Now it is only the expression of the minds of a few eccentric people.

Before our machine industrialism the word "art" meant *all* things made. Now it means just the few special things which they can't make by machinery—not yet.

(But of course they can make cheap machine-made reproductions of the "old masters" and they do a good trade in these.)

. . . . .

Now, it is quite obvious, this factory system, this industrialism is the natural expression of the financial domination under which we live, and which we all believe in. (For we are all in the same boat—the little shopkeeper and the little factory hand just as much as the big bankers and big industrialists, all believe in production for profit and all believe in labour-saving machinery and reducing the costs of production.)

Production for "profit"—that is the key phrase. We may ask: "Whose profit?" and the answer is clear—the profit of those who have invested money—the people commonly called "shareholders."

Formerly it was possible to say: *"the artist is not a special kind of man but every man is a special kind of artist."*

To-day such a saying is ridiculous, has no meaning. The artist is a very special kind of man and all other men are only expected to appreciate good things in their spare time—when they are not working.

When they are working, they are not artists because they are not responsible for what the machines make.

So the idea has grown up that culture is the product of leisure; and teachers and preachers and broadcasting corporations tell us that the working man must be educated to be cultured in his spare time.

.   .   .   .

So "art" has become a substitute for religion. Something you do in your spare time. Like church on Sundays. Nothing to do with the ordinary job of living. . . .

And so we have museums and art galleries, like temples in the middle of our cities—in the places where they used to build cathedrals.

.   .   .   .

So that is art in England, as it seems to me!

In brief: The majority of the people are degraded to the position of "hands"—instruments of profit to be supplanted by machines as soon as possible.

And the major part of what is *produced* is also degraded because it is no longer the product of human beings, producing things for use and giving a natural human affection to their work, but is the product of machines. And even this machine product is not primarily produced for use but is produced primarily for sale—for sale, that is to say, for profit.

Naturally things become degraded in this process. And on the other hand, and because of this degradation of ordinary necessary things, we give an exaggerated worship to the special things and to the remains of the past.

We pay fabulous prices for old pictures and even modern ones and we build magnificent temples to house the pots and pans of ancient Egypt or Palestine. And we exalt the special people called artists and give them quite unheard of and sentimental honour—making them Lords and Knights.

.   .   .   .   .

Of course, it is quite obvious, the only remedy for this state of things—if anybody wants a remedy—lies *in the sphere of ownership*.

The ownership of modern industry is the impersonal ownership of joint stock, limited liability companies. Under such auspices it is inevitable that production can only be for the sake of profit. In such a system good quality is all right, *if it pays*—not otherwise.

Production for use rather than for profit can only be an effective motive where ownership is personal rather than impersonal.

The rise of the merchant class in the fifteenth century and henceforth the domination of production by money motives has brought us to our present state.

Obviously the remedy is a *reversal* of the process—that is to say the supersession of financial ownership and control of production by the ownership and control of those who do the work rather than the selling. Naturally the salesman is a good servant but a bad master. Is it not plain common sense that good quality is best known by those who make things? People who live by buying cheap and selling dear can naturally not be expected to know a good thing from a bad one—they can only judge by the "balance sheet." And, on the other hand, the consumers, the people who buy, they cannot be expected to know good things from bad either. They also are governed by the money argument. And they are at the mercy of more or less untruthful advertisement.

And what applies to small workships or studios applies equally to large workshops and factories.

You can never get good poems or good paintings unless you give the final and absolute control to the personal judgment of the poet or painter. And you'll never get good household furniture or clothes or food or pottery or building materials unless you give the final and absolute control to the personal judgement of the workers in those various trades and take it away from the bankers and financiers and shareholders whose one criterion of judgement is the account books—the profits and the dividends.

In a word the ownership of the means of production must belong to the workers. At present it belongs to the banks and so we have only what *pays* and not what is *good*.

. . . . .

Ownership of the means of production by the workers! This sounds like Communism. What of it?

Pope Leo XIII said: "As many as possible of the people should be induced to become owners."

Apply this to our industrial society.

An individual man can own a small workshop and his tools; but an individual can't own a railway system and all the carriages and locomotives. Such a thing *must* be owned collectively.

At present railways and such giant enterprises are owned collectively by the shareholders, bondholders, financiers; and that is the worst possible kind of ownership because it means simply production for profit—can't mean anything else.

What I say is: railways and all our big industrial enterprises should be owned by those who work and are responsible for the working. This is personal ownership instead of the impersonal ownership of the joint stock companies.

Then we'll get production for use—not otherwise.

. . . . .

How to bring this about? That's not my present affair. Here

and now I am only concerned to state the truth—that those who do the work should own the means of working, and that ownership means personal control.

Here you may burst out (though I can't hear you) saying: but we thought you didn't believe in industrialism!

Well, suppose I don't. Even so, I ask in reply, how can you abolish something you don't control?

The first thing, in any case, is to get control of the thing. Then and then only shall we be in a position to break it up.

Who am I to say that people should not have railways and telephones and cinemas if they want them?

What I have the right to say and do say is that it is for the workers to decide—and they can't decide until they own.

Meanwhile there's nothing to stop us encouraging individual craftsmen wherever possible and desirable. Whatever happens, there will always be scope for such and when the rule of the profiteers is ended, individual craftsmen will cease to be their lap-dogs.

CHAPTER XII

ART AND BUSINESS

*(Introducing an exhibition of handicrafts arranged and held
by Messrs. Gane of Bristol)*

ART in the simplest and most universal sense of the word is "the well-making of what needs making." In the special sense in which it is often used to-day it means the expression of the sense of beauty. But during the many centuries of man's past history the two things went together and were not talked about. In the ordinary business of making things both the idea of making them well and the instinct for making them beautiful were united. But in the last 150 years, since the introduction of the factory system and the development of machinery, the idea that the workman was responsible for making things well and that in the course of so doing he would naturally satisfy his sense of beauty has disappeared in the trades which supply the necessaries of life—food, clothing, furniture and utensils—and it only persists in the trades which, because they are not capable of being organized in factories and mechanized, are still carried on by individual persons working for their own personal customers. The ordinary workman has been reduced in status and is now generally looked upon as an irresponsible "hand," doing only what he is told to do or what the machine requires. And the special workman has been raised to an abnormally high position and has become simply a purveyor of luxuries for rich people.

Historically this state of affairs was never seen in the world before. The result of Industrialism (factories and machines) has been to multiply the necessaries of life exceedingly and to reduce the number of things which we regard as beautiful. It has also greatly increased the number of salesmen, who do not make things but only sell them (with little knowledge). So we have the designer who designs what he never makes and the worker who minds the machine which makes what he never designs. And we have the salesman who neither designs things nor minds machines but is supposed to know what the public wants. But the public doesn't know what it wants, and it has no means of finding out. So people are dependent upon the salesman and the salesman is only concerned with what will sell. Saleability is his only criterion—if a thing sells it is good and if it won't sell it is bad—or at any rate, not worth making.

This is a bad state of affairs, as most people will admit. For though we have many more things than we used to have, few of them are really well made and none of them is worth keeping. They have none of the venerable or holy quality which things used to have—the quality which makes us treasure them and put them in museums. And so, though the first object of making things is to serve one another, we do not serve one another well. And we are forced to comfort ourselves with quantity because we cannot get quality.

Now there are all sorts of causes for this bad state of affairs, but we are not concerned with causes here. The point here is that one of the main reasons why things are bad is that the men who make them are not responsible. If you go to a shop to buy something it is generally impossible to find the person who made it. There isn't anyone. Nobody can be praised and nobody can be blamed. The whole system is quite impersonal. The workers only mind the machines. The machine-makers only take instructions from the designers. The designers take instructions from the salesmen. The salesmen are simply the servants of the investors.

And the investors are only interested in dividends. You see it is a hopeless mess. So what?

Well, without going into the politics of the matter, or, deeper still, the religious causes of the trouble, there are some things which might be done. Everybody suspects advertisements, and everybody knows that the salesman as such is not a judge of what is good in itself. But everybody, just because he is human, prefers good quality to bad. How can we find good things? What guarantee can we obtain that things are well made and at a just price?

The first thing to do is, whenever possible, to buy things from the actual makers or from the shop where they are actually made. That is to say: The first thing is to re-establish the personal relationship between maker and buyer. The buyer knows the use of things and therefore he has the best reasons for knowing his needs. The maker knows how to make things—what else is he for? —and therefore he has the best reasons for claiming to be able to satisfy the needs of the buyer.

The shop is the place where the maker displays his goods, and it is the place where the buyer can most conveniently inspect them—it is the meeting place of maker and buyer. That is its proper function. The shopkeeper provides this meeting place. That is *his* function—he is the servant of both buyer and maker. If we could again establish shops where the goods for sale were made by the same firm and as far as possible on the same premises, and if the manufacturing side of the business were again given its proper primacy and responsibility—the selling side being honourably humble and subordinate—then we should be well on the way to the revival of that craftsmanship and beauty of design for which British manufactures were formerly famous.

CHAPTER XIII

THE HUMAN PERSON AND SOCIETY

(Written for a series of pamphlets entitled The Bond of Peace)

IT HAS been obvious for a long time, perhaps from its beginning, that the Peace Pledge Union is a movement and an organization of people who are not merely anti-war or anti-violence. It is obvious that the peace pledge, in spite of the simple negative in which it is expressed, implies much more than the simple determination to refuse military service, to oppose conscription and preach a gospel of non-violence. For every negative implies a positive; the very refusal to do such and such a thing implies a determination, or at least a wish, to do something else. Abstinence from a course of action which seems evil in itself or evil as being a bad or ineffectual method of gaining something good, does not imply a life of inaction. Not even the ancient or modern hermit who seems to his fellow-men to be simply running away from life and activity, not even the total abstainer from alcoholic drink, not even the celibate priest or pious virgin—none of these has taken a vow of abstinence except as being the first step towards some positive activity to which life "in the world" or "strong drink" or marriage was or seemed a hindrance. And this is true of all asceticism, even of that which is practised by professional footballers or boxers. Asceticism means training, for the sake of a positive good. And if this be true when good things are given up for the sake of something better, how much more true it is when an evil thing, a thing admitted by everybody to be evil, a thing which, as Mr. Neville Chamberlain has said, "gains nothing, settles nothing," war, is denied and refused?

It is true, therefore, that the Peace Pledge does not mean simply a hatred of war, even of war in the sub-human and worse-than-bestial form which it must necessarily take to-day; it implies a realization that physical war of any kind is a bad means to the winning of the kind of world that men really want, the kind of world which really fits their human nature. It is that world, that human world, that world of men at peace which is implied by our refusal to take part in war. Pacifism is a positive thing; that is the point. It is a point insufficiently grasped by us and not grasped at all by our critics. That is why these pamphlets are being written.

. . . . .

Pacifism is a positive faith; it is the faith of those who believe that men are made for peace and that peace is not only natural to men but is that state of affairs in which alone men can fulfil themselves or (which is only another way of saying the same thing) properly serve their fellow-men and love and praise God. "Peace is the tranquillity of order"; it is that order for which the Peace Pledge is the necessary first step—the first step which is necessary to clear the deck for action. The Peace Pledge Union has not failed because it has failed to prevent war—the war that is now upon us. The Peace Pledge Union will only have failed when it ceases to make pacifists. Its real and primary work is not the prevention of war, necessary though that work is; its primary and real work is the preparation of peace, the rediscovery of the foundations of human order and the winning of men to build upon them.

. . . . .

Human order—what is human, what is man? It seems easy to answer these questions, and we are so prone to acceptance of the notion of the world which nineteenth-century scientists put before us, that we are all willing to give easy answers. We measure men and observe their behaviour; we collect statistics and tabulate men's habits and appetites; and we fail to see that the notion of man thus arrived at leaves out all that men most value in one another and leaves in only that information and those particulars which are of value to his enemies. "A man's enemies are those of his own household"; man's inhumanity to man is the chief trouble, and that trouble, prevalent enough in all times and places, is accentuated to-day and enormously increased by a way of thinking and a way of working which are false to man's nature. We have abandoned the corruptions of princely and ecclesiastical rule only to fall headlong into the anti-human rule of financiers and men of commerce with all their sub-human and non-human methods of mass production, instituted not, as they vainly boast, for the sake of social amenity but solely for their own riches and private aggrandizement.

Let us be quite clear about it. Ill-will is the first possible sin; but ill-will is supported and defended by false thought. First of all we are selfish and then we talk about "enlightened self-interest"! It is that enlightenment which is now our darkness. It is false thinking about man which is now our first enemy.

What is human, what is man? Man is matter and spirit—both real and both good. And what is this creature thus compounded? He is a person. That is the point, the first thing to be said, the first thing we know. And we know it first from our own experience of ourselves and of our fellow-men and women and not because we have been taught it by scientific lecturers or read about it in books. A person, a being who knows and wills and loves, who is responsible for his acts and for the intended consequences of his acts; a being who, because he is responsible, is able to be damned, who merits praise or blame; a rational creature knowing, by the light of his nature, true and false, good and evil, right and wrong—not wholly or infallibly but sufficiently—and, above all, a creature who loves—not merely with the seeming obsequiousness of tame beasts which scarcely know or will, but with the willing devotion and self-sacrifice of beings who know in *whom* they believe. That is briefly what we mean by the word person. It is no philosophical invention, no abstraction, nothing which either microscope or telescope could reveal; it is that which we know ourselves to be.

Man is matter and spirit—neither one nor the other, but both, inseparable, conjoined and commixed. Up and down the world from the beginning of man's history he has stumbled over this paradox and has endeavoured to escape. Frightened by its lusts, he has sworn enmity to his own body. Dismayed by apparitions and by revelations, true or false, and angered by the weakness of religious men and their betrayal of their own precepts, he has vowed himself an enemy of the spirit and of religion—a rule or way of life purporting to be laid upon him from outside and from above. So on the one hand, all the puritanisms, from Arius, and before Arius, to Aldous Huxley—those who say that the spirit alone is man's true life—and, on the other, all the paganisms, from Babylon, and before Babylon, to Rome of the Caesars, Rome of the Renaissance, to the Paris, London and New York of to-day. So also, to-day, those mixtures of puritanism and paganism, which we know as Communism and Fascism and Nazism—violent revolts against the religion of Christianity which Christians have betrayed and violent revolts against the wickedness and corruption of the wild individualism which made public service a means to private profit.

Man is matter and spirit. In their endeavour to escape the entanglement of material lust men have declared matter to be evil. In their endeavour to put the house of this world in order, to deal with the material and bodily needs of men and women and children, needs to which the lords of money and manufacture have been blind; needs which men of religion, in their obsequiousness to the mammon to which they looked for support, have neglected; men have declared religion to be unnecessary and merely the opium of the people, a means of keeping the masses in subservience to lords and masters. All these things are understandable and forgivable. But the truth remains: man is matter and spirit—both real and both good, and escape is impossible. Salvation, the salvation of men, and that is to say the wholeness, and that again is to say the *holiness* of men, is not attainable by denying either side or component of his nature. The only question is: which shall rule? And to this question there can be only one answer. Man is matter and spirit, but the primacy is of the spirit. And here again we are not saying anything learnt merely from a text-book or by means of scientific inquiry. The primacy of the spirit is a fact of our experience. We know ourselves as persons and therefore as governed, ruled, ordered and led (however often we have been or are misled) by our personal selves. We may and must allow its due weight to the physical and material world which conditions our lives, and all its geological, geographical, climatic, racial and economic forces and circumstances; but those things did not make us; they are simply the conditions under and in which we live. We neglect or deny them at our peril; but to deny our spiritual nature and its primacy is not merely dangerous, it is man's damnation. The integrity of the individual means exactly that—the realization of man's dual nature and the primacy of the spirit.

Now the nature of man is not seen only in each individual person; it is seen also in the groups or collections of men which we call societies or nations. For man, the animal man, is a social animal and however much, in some moods of discontent with and rebellion against our surroundings, we may imagine ourselves to be self-sufficient and may yearn for the simple, self-sufficing life of Robinson Crusoe, yet even if it be only for the sake of procreation, we need and depend upon the company and collaboration of our fellows. But procreation means the family—father, mother, children—and no two persons are alike; our talents and powers are different. Thus we develop different functions and thus we develop not only ourselves but also the society. The advantages of the co-operation of persons differently talented are obvious; the point here is that we are dependent upon one another and cannot live alone. We are therefore members one of another, members of one body, and though we may choose to allow the private guard-ianship and custody and use of property to individual persons, and call it the "institution of property," such proprietorship is not in reality, nor can it ever be an absolute ownership. It is and must be an ownership subject to *the common good*.

Consider the development of industry with which we are fa-miliar to-day. A man may very well "own" a horse and cart, his own horse, his own cart; and he may very well set up a carrier's business, dealing personally with his personal customers. No harm is done to anyone if he be proud of his horse and paint his cart with his own name, and, if he be a just man and the idea of justice pervade the society in which he lives and works (justice: the ren-dering of equivalents, the striking of a balance), there is no reason to suppose that the natural animal propensity to take rather than to give cannot be duly curbed and subjected to the common good. But it is clear that no such line of thinking can apply to the giant organizations we call Railway Companies. The ownership of such affairs has long since ceased to be in any way personal. It has become the entirely impersonal and therefore irresponsible owner-ship of vast conglomerations of anonymous investors whose only interest, as they more or less freely admit,[1] is in the dividend or share of the profits which a combination of luxuries for travellers and underpayment of employees can effect. And the same is true of all the giant commercial undertakings of our time. Public serv-ices are owned and run for private profit. Thus masses of men are driven to discontent and revolt and the common good is neg-lected, forgotten and denied. These giant concerns were in their origins the product of individual initiative and adventure and genius for invention and organization. But the due reward of such individual prowess has long since been over-reached, and now, at last, in our time, such are the vast opportunities of profit to be derived from this system of anonymous investment, it has come about that we commonly judge a man great and good not

[1] See publications of the British Railway Stockholders Union and compare letter of Sir Percy Bates, *The Times*, 15th January, 1936.

by reason of his disinterested service but, on the contrary, by the success with which he has been able to exploit his fellows. Is it surprising that on all sides there should be discontent, disillusion, and revolt at home and, because such methods of commerce have led to the world-wide development of machinery and the consequent feverish competition for markets for the sale of the mass of things produced, is it surprising that there should be war abroad? (Not because men of business desire it, but because war is the inevitable consequence of their ignorance and malice—it is the scourge of God.)

Moreover this system of money rule, Capitalism, with machine mass-production, and salesmanship as its one means of continuance, and saleability as its one criterion of good, Capitalism inevitably places the phenomenon of surplus production in an entirely new and evil light. Leisure, leisure for recreation, which should be man's delight, leisure whose proper object is that men should return to work refreshed and revived, leisure has become an idol. For work, the means to living, has become hateful and degrading, and leisure instead of being the means has become the end. Food, clothing and shelter, the necessaries of life, the things which throughout man's history have been those in which he has chiefly delighted and delighted to express himself [1] and also those through which and by means of which he has expressed his unity with the universe and his creativeness, his love of his fellow-men and his love of God, his delight in the physical world and his ability to collaborate with God in creating, these things have, quite literally, been reduced to the sphere of the drains—necessaries of physical life, not holy and venerable such as those works of our fathers which we now place in museums; necessaries of life, objects of commerce, things to sell. And, such are our methods, those who mind the machines which make things are not in any way responsible for the form and quality of what the machines turn out. Reduced to "a sub-human

---

[1] But note: self-expression is not, as the aestheticians hold, the *object* of personal work; it is but its natural accident and accompaniment—to be curbed rather than belauded. Mutual aid and the praise of God are the proper objects.

condition of intellectual irresponsibility," they are concerned only with the wages they draw and the improvement of the physical conditions under which they labour. Hence, on the one hand, a desire for shorter hours of work and longer leisure, and on the other a dread of the unemployment which the capitalist control of industry inevitably produces.

Again let us be clear about it. Surplus production is no new phenomenon. There has always been a surplus. Nature, by which we now mean the physical world, nature itself produces a surplus; a surplus is a necessity of natural life. Take the ordinary potato! Plant one potato and ten or more come up. Upon that fact the whole edifice of human society is built. The problem is not how to avoid a surplus but how to utilize and distribute it. Were it not for the fact that the husbandman can grow vastly more food than he and his family can consume, our civilization, with all its differentiation of trades and services, could never have existed. Man is a person—matter and spirit. His body is made of the earth. The food he eats is the very material of his flesh. His flesh, his blood, his bones are actually made of grass. The earth's green mantle is not only his carpet—it is his very body. And it produces a surplus. Men cannot eat all the food they grow. Of necessity they must either lie about in idleness or do something else besides husbandry. But idleness does not suit his spirit. That is the trouble. Few there are who can contemplate the divine mystery of existence and do nothing about it. Some are called to a life of pure contemplation, but how few! And even the pious hermit must spend some time and labour to provide food for himself. Most of us are called to action as well as contemplation and to action which is the fruit of contemplation. But no one is called to action pure and simple.

It would occupy many books to deal adequately with this matter. Here we are only concerned to epitomize, to give a general view. For, in the complexity of our civilization, our townized industrial capitalism, with its excessive differentiation and specialization and (such is one of the results of our concentration upon salesmanship) its almost complete absence of veracious information (the sale of news is one of the most profitable sources of "dividends"), a general view of man's life and its meaning is of all things the most hard to come by. And in a general view of man's life on this planet, this green earth, the first general truth is this: Man is matter and spirit. As a material creature he is made of the earth. As a spiritual being he is called to action, and the earth in its exuberance produces a surplus of food for his body, thus supplying him with the means for countless complexities of activity. And a general view of man's history shows us that only for two things has he ever sacrificed himself—patriotism and religion, either or both, together or separately. Never has he laid down his life for money, for "business." [1]

The earth produces a surplus. How shall that surplus be distributed? by whom shall it be used? Men of action and men of contemplation, each have swayed the world, and each individual man is compounded of both. All our civilizations are to be seen in these terms. Patriotism, the honour and aggrandizement of our country, religion, the honour and aggrandizement of our very being—Patriotism and Religion, Religion and Patriotism, these two things command and have obtained our allegiance and our blood. Never until our time have men founded their societies upon any other bases. But capitalism, that historical monstrosity, is a thing independent of either. It is the proud achievement of capitalists that they have made religion unnecessary. Religion is nothing to do with business. Religion is your private affair. Religion means going to your particular conventicle on Sundays and forgetting about it for the rest of the week. And this not at all because men of business are hypocrites, but because they firmly believe that Religion is unnecessary in public affairs. And Patriotism! Patriotism is nothing to do with business either. Business means selling

[1] Money, not gold or silver or treasure—men have often given or at least risked their lives for these, and war in its prehistoric beginnings was simply robbery and raiding of the haves by the have-nots (hence the defence of riches and possessions became a "patriotic" duty). No, by money I mean "business," investments, dividends, and the whole capitalist caboodle.

things—what has patriotism got to do with that? What does it matter who buys so long as those who buy can pay? And war? Patriotism and war have never in man's long history been separated. What has war to do with business unless you happen to be selling armaments? It is not the business man who is the patriot, though he has often found it profitable to exploit the patriotism of other men. It is not the business man who is the warrior and war is bad business on all accounts, for it hinders trade and kills thousands of those who might buy. The internationalism of finance and of commercial companies [1] shows clearly that patriotism has nothing to do with business and business men are only interested in war when war happens to be profitable. And if it might seem that certain business interests are in favour of war in Europe to-day that is only because the politics of certain European countries are or seem to be inimical to business—business as run by capitalists, capitalism itself. Whatever the confusion of our politics and the mendacity of our newspapers, it is clear that the whole capitalist notion is to get people into debt and debt is only possible as the result of sales.[2]

Production is the business of capitalism; for production means things to sell—the more the better. War, however profitable to those who sell munitions, means destruction, and that is why it is so desperately necessary to make it appear to the ordinary man that it is being fought for justice and the honour of his country. It is not because capitalism has won that we are at war to-day; but because capitalism has failed. It has failed, as they say, to deliver the goods. It has not given prosperity and plenty to all, but only to the few. It has very nearly destroyed religion; but it has not given man happiness here or promise of happiness hereafter. It has very nearly destroyed patriotism; for it has ruined the country, the land, turned it into a morass of overgrown and vulgar cities; it has destroyed the people, reduced us in our millions to

---

[1] E.g., Unilever, the I.C.I. and the armament firms themselves!
[2] Debt! But not of course that kind of debt which harasses the poor, but that kind of debt which is represented by double entry book-keeping.

a mass of irresponsible factory-hands with no love of our work, no hope of happiness except through the false excitement of cheap cinemas and cheap "radio," no power to amuse ourselves either in work or play, and thrown millions of us out of employment altogether—a scrap-heap and refuse dump of unwanted beings, persons, human souls, creatures who know and will and love, but who know no wisdom, have no opportunity to exercise their wills and have nothing to love but one another's bodies, and only those bodies provided that we remain barren, plant no seed and bear no fruit. The war of to-day is not really the product of men of business; it is the inevitable reaction of a world in which business has failed.

Patriotism and Religion. These always have been and always will be the only things for which men will sacrifice themselves, their possessions, their money. The exuberance of nature, the surplus product, the activity of the animal and spiritual man— these can only find employment in patriotism or faith. The capitalist idea was to corner the surplus and put it up for sale. It has done so and the world cannot buy. It is finished. The alternatives are before us. If you do not turn the surplus into commodities for sale, the natural surplus, the inevitable surplus, then you must use it for enjoyment or for destruction—for religion or for war.

We all know how the surplus is and was used in war; we have forgotten how it was and how it might be used in faith. But look at past history! Even those who are so enamoured of our mechanical triumphs (and indeed they are triumphs) as to deny that the past has any exemplary value, will not deny its value as a source of information. Rome, Egypt, Assyria, Mexico, India, China, our own Middle Ages—all those places and periods show us the way in which the human race used the natural surplus before the capitalist idea of reinvestment came in to minister to our animal greed. The great monuments of past cultures give us their answers. Neither the unemployment of capitalism nor the destruction of war is necessary—the activity of man and his spiritual enthusiasm can be expended in the service of his Gods! We may laugh or we may sneer; but in this place it is only necessary to note the facts, the actual physical facts. The ruins of their monuments cannot lie. Whether it was churches or temples, bridges or tombs of kings or whether it was only in the fineness or goodness of their clothes and domestic furniture, it was in that way that they expended the surplus of exuberant nature.

But under business government the surplus is disused, it goes to rot or is thrown into the sea and, in human terms, it is unemployed, rotting on "the dole." Which shall we choose then, war or religion—which shall we choose of these? Capitalist disuse is coming rapidly to its natural end. There remain religious use and militarist misuse, and religion and war are ultimately incompatible.

We know well enough the virtues that are promoted in war— courage, self-sacrifice, brotherhood, constancy. We know well enough the contrary vices which war promotes no less. But who will dare to say that courage is not needed in any human life; and are not self-sacrifice and brotherhood and constancy precisely the virtues inculcated by religion? It is the world of business which saps men's virtue, which turns us all into black-coated rabbits hardly able to be damned. In an ordinary normal human life, in which men of business are subordinate, there is need for the virtue of courage on every hand. The ordinary trades are not carried on in quilted waistcoats. Men's bodies, before machinery made labour seem despicable, had to be strong; and self-reliance and initiative were the pride of every craftsman. The brotherhood of men, affirmed in the Gospel, was reaffirmed by every guild; and who can count the number of those who have suffered for conscience sake? Such argument in favour of war is specious and superficial—specious because war to-day, the mechanized, sub-human affair we still call by that ancient name, has very nearly done away the heroic quality of the little wars of the past ("Cannon-fodder" is no empty taunt), and superficial because it is only concerned with the outward seeming of the business and leaves untouched the world-wide damage war does to the human race, to the souls of men and to the Body of which we are members.

Let us return, in conclusion, to that point. This is not primarily an anti-militarist tract. Our business here is to affirm certain things about the human person and the relation of men to one another. In the stink and confusion of our time we are confronted by two main and commanding ideas of society—democracy [1] and totalitarianism, the failure of one leading to the acceptance and even the inevitability of the other. Democracy has failed. But why? But how? Men are responsible beings, responsible for their actions, responsible for their works; how then, and why, should it not be right and proper and possible for them to govern themselves? The answer should be plain to us. Democracy has failed—but only because it has been stolen and diverted from its proper object, the common good, and made the instrument for the destruction of the very things it was to preserve. The integrity of the individual person, the freedom of the workman to choose his way of work and his responsibility for what he produces, the freedom of men and women to marry and have children and their responsibility for their children's education and nurture, the real responsibility of men for the choosing of leaders and governors— these things democracy was to promote and preserve, these things have been degraded and destroyed. If England is not already a totalitarian state it is only because financial and commercial oligarchs have up to the present found it possible to stave it off. For totalitarianism, enemy of democracy though it be, is also the enemy of the princes of commerce; it is, like democracy, and by definition, concerned for the common good, and to many it seems the only way out of the quagmire, the dirty mess of capitalism. Peace is the tranquillity of order. The disorder of our society leads to the reaction in favour of the cast-iron order of totalitarianism.

[1] Democracy, not in the sense of the newspapers, viz., "government by parliamentary oligarchies" ruling what is virtually a servile state. In our view democracy is impossible unless the people be free, and freedom is impossible in our (or any other) capitalist industrialism. What we mean by democracy is *not* what we have got at present but "government of free men and free families developing through guilds and corporations and real control of their own and their country's affairs."

Private property had led to every kind of injustice; let us therefore all be proletarians, say the Communists. The churches have everywhere sided with the tyrants and served only to dope the people; let us abolish God! The selfishness of financiers and men of commerce and the supineness of princes have betrayed the people to unemployment and misery; let us abandon the hope of democracy and all its moribund parliaments and set the state in order by direct action from above, say the totalitarians. Reaction, reaction, always reaction! Always a violent swing to the opposite extreme, never a quiet mind, never wisdom—the knowledge of things in their ultimate causes. But if our plutocracy destroys the person, totalitarianism denies it. It is in this dilemma that we find ourselves. This is the cleft stick in which man is likely to be caught. It is this crisis of our history in which the Peace Pledge Union, by its affirmation of the supreme value of the human person, is determined to make a stand. The human way, therefore the way of persons. The human way, therefore the way of brothers. The human way, therefore the way of freemen and not that of the beehive. The human way, therefore the way of Christ.

CHAPTER XIV

ART

I

"Art is not an aesthetic but a rhetorical activity."

ANANDA COOMARASWAMY.

THE Incarnation may be said to have for Its object the drawing of men from misery to happiness. Being the act of God It is the greatest of all rhetorical acts and therefore the greatest of all works of art. And as from the fatherhood of God all paternity is named in heaven and earth, so from His creative power all art is named. In the Incarnation we do not only know a fact of history or a truth of religion; we behold a work of art, a thing *made*. As a fact of history It is the most interesting and illuminating of all historical happenings. As a truth of religion It is of primary and fundamental importance. But it is as a work of art that It has saving power, power to persuade, power to heal, power to rescue, power to redeem.

But the word "art," in spite of the obsequious worship which the modern world gives to the works of painters and sculptors and musicians, is not a holy word in these days. Art, the word, which primarily means skill and thus human skill in doing and making, has, in literary circles and among the upper classes, come to mean only the fine arts, and the fine arts have ceased to be rhetorical and are now exclusively aesthetic; they aim only to give pleasure.

Hence, however cultured we may be and however refined our pleasures, we do not associate the word with holiness, or holiness with art. If we associate holiness with art at all it is only with that lowest form of art, the "holy picture," the cheap mass-produced reproductions we distribute as pious gestures. But art, "high art," the sort we put in museums and picture galleries, has become a pleasure thing; it is put there to amuse. Eat, drink, and be merry for to-morrow we die, and the utmost endeavour of our educators, is to see to it that our merriment shall be "high class." If we put a painting of the Madonna in our art gallery it is not because the painter has succeeded in conveying a specially clear view of her significance, but simply because he has succeeded in making a specially pleasing arrangement of materials. A Raphael Madonna! But it is as "Raphael" that we honour it and not as a Madonna; for Raphael is, or was until recently, held by the pundits to be particularly good at making pleasing arrangements, and we are no longer concerned with meanings.

But "in the beginning was a thought, not a thing," and therefore it is that intelligibility is the final cause of all thing. "Pleasure perfects the operation," but is not the object of working. Final happiness consists in the joy of knowing and not in the satisfaction of sense however refined. Nevertheless, we must not under-value or eschew pleasure as though it were evil. On the contrary, exactly as in our physical life, in eating and drinking and all other bodily activities, when there is no pleasure in the work we know there is something wrong with it, and when there is nothing pleasing in the result we know it has been badly done, so it is with things made—pleasure perfects the operation. And there is even pleasure in pain when the pain is the necessary accompaniment or companion of good work. Thus there is satisfaction in the pain of ordinary physical labour and, in the heights of holiness, there is pleasure in the agony of maternity and of martyrdom. "A man should have joy in his labour," says the Preacher, "and this is his portion"; nevertheless, art remains a rhetorical and not an aesthetic activity.

"That while we know God by sight, we may be drawn by Him to the love of things unseen. . . ." "and the Word was made flesh." It is clear, therefore, that it is as a thing made, a thing seen, a thing known precisely because thus made and seen, that we must first of all consider the Incarnation. "That we may be drawn"; in these words [1] the rhetorical nature of the life and work of Our Lord, and therefore its nature as a work of art is stated. And the applications should be clear also. Man is a social animal. He is not self-sufficient. He cannot live without his neighbours; they cannot live without him. But the object of life is "your sanctification." Therefore all our neighbourliness must have that end in view, and therefore we are all evangelists and all our works are in their true nature evangelical; they have for their object, their final cause, their end, the winning of beatitude; for each man his own beatitude and for each man the beatitudes of his friends and neighbours; my own greatest happiness and enjoyment, yes; the greatest happiness of the greatest number, yes; to be happy with Him eternally.

In these statements I am merely stating facts; such and such is the nature of our life and of our work. But it is necessary to avoid the implication that because all work is of its nature evangelical that therefore we must always be consciously thinking of it as such. Provided that we know it to be so and order our lives accordingly, we may well forget all about it. We may even suppose Our Lord, though always "about My Father's business," was not always discursively thinking of it. "He prays best," said St. Anthony of the desert, "who does not know that he is praying." And, similarly, he preaches best who does not know that he is preaching and, even, he loves best who does not know that he is loving. And thus we may go on to say that those works are best which are not labelled holy, which are holy in their nature and without advertisement. The Gospels make a holy book, the most successfully rhetorical of all books, but they are not sicklied o'er with the

1 But the word "drawn" is not strong enough. The Latin is *rapiamur*. The sight of Him is ravishing, not attractive merely.

pale cast of religiosity; a mere literary man can enjoy them and not know that he is being "got at." We may suspect that our Lord's life was the same; when we meet Him we are not embarrassed and repelled by his self-conscious piety.

It should be clear, therefore, that in proclaiming the essentially evangelical nature of all human works we are not suggesting that the whole world ought to turn itself into one great "church furniture" shop. The contrary would be nearer the truth, we ought rather to abolish church furniture shops altogether; for just as prayer almost ceases to be prayer when we know that we are praying, so "church" art ceases to be suitable for churches. The whole point is that human works should be holy, for holiness is properly their criterion, and holiness is not simply that which is so called.

II

"The invisible things of God may be clearly seen, being understood by the things which are made."

The Word was made flesh; that is to say: "the day-spring from on high has visited us," and in our works we reach nearest to that highness when, in a manner of speaking, we carry on that visitation. But we are not to suppose that because pictures and sculptures and poetry are or may be more explicitly rhetorical than chairs and tables that there is or need be any greater holiness in works of fine art than in other works. We know God by sight in the person of our Lord, but we know him by sight in and through *all* His works. When God looked at the world of His creation "He saw that it was good." But "one alone is good," God Himself. Therefore God sees Himself reflected in His creation, and we also may see Him thus. His creation is not Himself but it is His word, not *the* Word but *His* word, a word that we may hear.

> . . . *emittit eloquium suum terrae;*
> *velociter currit sermo ejus.*

Thus again we are confronted by a rhetorical activity. In His creation God invites our attention, draws us to Him, craves our love. And we may carry on the same work; we may collaborate with Him in creating.

That is the difference between art and science. Science is analytical, descriptive, informative. Man does not live by bread alone, but by science he attempts to do so. Hence the deadliness of all that is purely scientific. "Industry without art is brutality," said John Ruskin. And it is for this reason that through science and the industries to which science has been rigorously applied we approach rather the works of the brutes than of men. The work of the bee building its comb is simply the application of science to industry. Whether done by what we call instinct or by conscious calculation there is no difference in the nature of the work. In either case only that is done which is demanded by the physical necessities of the occasion. This is not to say that the work of scientists and scientific workers (engineers, mechanics, chemists, financiers) is despicable, on the contrary, it is admirable, as admirable as that of bees and ants; and bicycles and wireless sets, when they are truly themselves and not camouflaged to look like human works, arouse in us the same admiration as do our own livers and lights—wonderful contrivances, ingenious apparatuses, but essentially brutal in kind.

Here it will be thought that writing as an artist I have no proper respect for other sorts of works. But it should be noted that I am not claiming a special loftiness for a small class of special persons for, in a normal society, one, that is to say, composed of responsible persons, responsible for what they do and for what they make, "the artist is not a special kind of man, but every man is a special kind of artist." There is no such hard distinction between the fine arts and others as there is in modern England, and therefore there is no such hard distinction between what is useful physically and what is useful mentally. In such a society if science and its applications were less worshipped, for it and they would be less profitable, so also would art and artists be, for it and they would have ceased to be eccentric. Artists no less than

Scientists have got to come off their high horses. The fact remains: art is a normal human activity as scientifically controlled industry is not; for making things by human means for human use is the normal occupation of human beings, while the quantitative mass-production methods which are the natural consequence of the scientific method are in their nature abnormal and sub-human. Art as a virtue of the practical intelligence is the well-making of what is needed—whether it be drain-pipes or paintings and sculptures and musical symphonies of the highest religious import—and science is that which enables us to deal faithfully with technique. As art is the handmaid of religion, science is the handmaid of art.[1]

What is the rhetorical value of a mass-produced teapot? To what end does it lead? Such questions are difficult to answer. It is useless to say a man can be a very good Catholic in a factory. That won't help him to give rhetorical value to the work he does "on the belt." And for the same reason it is useless to say that science has alleviated much physical pain and labour; moreover for one pain alleviated, scientifically controlled industry has brought into existence ten pains and miseries or a hundred that did not previously exist. Not all our skill in surgery and medicine can compensate for the dehumanization and depersonalization of life that industrialism necessarily connotes, or the unholiness of industrial products. It is not easy to describe a negative. Bad is the privation of good; unholiness is the privation of holiness. On the other hand, neither is it easy to say precisely in what the goodness, the sanctity of pre-industrial or non-industrial things consists. All industrial products, however saleable, however flat-

---

[1] Incidentally, we should escape such monstrosities as Renaissance architecture which, for all its charm, is simply theatrical flattery of human vanity on the one hand, and, on the other, is woefully devoid of scientific intelligence. We are mightily pleased when we see St. Peter's dome or the dome of St. Paul's, and are not aware of the chains that bind them round, and the innumerable sacrifices of good construction made by their architects for the sake of dramatic appearance. We should avoid the absurdity of machine-made ornamentation and the indecency of sprawling wens like London; and painters and sculptors, who, under our present financier-run tyranny, are compelled to be simply mountebanks or lap-dogs, and their works a sort of hot-house flowers, would again find themselves in normal employment as members of a building gang.

tering to our vanity, however useful in an ephemeral sort of way, are in their nature unholy or, if it will ease the reader's mind, lacking in holiness, but not all the works of men in other periods, not all the works of men outside the factory system are holy. There has always been much bad work done; for there have always been selfishness and vanity and greed, and there have always been stupidity and insensitiveness and foolish nonsense. But there is at least this distinction between industrialism and human labour: in the former, holiness is ruled out both from the life and the work; in the latter, holiness is a constant potentiality. And so it is that, in spite of the much bad work done in medieval England, or China or Peru, we may see constantly breaking out, so to say, those qualities which I group together under the general name of holiness. We are reluctant to admit these things, we are so enthralled by our material successes, but we are not reluctant to fill our museums and galleries with specimens of Chinese pottery, ancient cottage nick-nacks, and paintings and sculptures of all races and ages. We are not all aesthetes, doting on lines and colours and the relations of masses. We are not all archaeologians, talking about dates and the history of cultures. "That which being seen, pleases," yes. And we are all capable of pleasure; it is part of our equipment, for pleasure of the mind attracts us to the truth. We are social animals, and we are all interested in history. But it is not aesthetics or ancient history that endears things to us.

Endears! Perhaps that word may be a key for us. But I do not mean a sentimental endearment such as that which prompts us to treasure a child's lock of hair, or Ruskin's blue "tie" in a museum; I mean such endearment as pertains to the intrinsic quality of things. It is difficult to separate the sentimental from the intrinsic, and it is better so; for to be devoid of sentiment is to be inhuman and even ungodly. But there is no need to separate them. What is important is that we should keep things in their proper hierarchy. Man is a matter and spirit, and the primacy is the spirit. There is no formula for good works, whether of doing or making. It is the meaning that matters, and the meaning of the Universe is Emmanuel, God with us.

Apply it how you like. And it applies in all times and places. It is not only the Christians who have lived with God. Though we know Him "by sight," others have lived with Him in close and intimate "correspondence," and *we* have often turned away our eyes.

What is the rhetorical value of a teapot? In what way can a teapot minister to salvation? Here it becomes obvious that the word rhetoric does not simply mean verbal eloquence or didacticism.[1] And as he prays best who does not know that he is praying, so that craftsman ministers best who does not know that he is ministering. All that is required is that he shall be a responsible workman. As such he may contribute to the good life and the good life is that which leads heavenwards. There is no need that we should all be self-conscious prigs. There is no need to rule out gaiety or bodily enjoyment or even buffoonery, and we should learn to appreciate what we may call God's own coarse humour. God is no more refined than He is a "South Place" ethicist. Nature "red in tooth and claw" is as much in accord with His will as small children singing hymns. Rocky mountains, grassy downs, rats, germs, and dung, all are things singing to us of Him; and when we slip on an orange peel we may suppose He enjoys our laughter.

Art is a rhetorical activity—this is easily understood when we think of books and dramatic plays, of poetry and music, of pictures and sculptures. And if we realize that there is no dividing line between such things and the work of blacksmiths and navvies, we shall see how all things work together for good and that is to say, for God.

"I asked the earth and it said: 'I am not He,' and all things that are in the earth confessed the same. I asked the sea, the deeps,

---

[1] "Rhetoric or Oratory, in which eloquence is thought of not as an end in itself or art for art's sake, or to display the artist's skill, but as *effective communication*" (my italics).—Coomaraswamy.

and all creeping things and they answered: 'We are not your God, seek Him above us.' I asked the subtle air, and with all its inhabitants this air made answer: 'Anaximenes is deceived, I am not your God.' I asked the heavens, the sun, the moon, the stars. 'Neither are we,' said they, 'the God you seek.' And to all they who stood before those portals of my soul, my senses five, I said: 'As to my God, you say you are not He; but tell me now somewhat of what He is?' And with a mighty voice did they cry out: 'It is He that made us.' " (Confessions of St Augustine, Book X.)

Dante speaks to us of God, and so do the daisies, the dew-drops, and the dung. And if that is so, is it not even more obvious that pots and pans may do so? For the works of men and women carry the work of creation on to a higher level than that of what we call Nature. We are ourselves creators. Through us exist things which God Himself could not otherwise have made. The "natural" world is God's present to Himself. Our works are His works, but they are also in a strict sense our own, and if we present them to Him they are *our* presents to Him, and not simply His to Himself. They are free-will offerings. And, indeed, all things should thus be offered up. There is, properly, no such thing as a secular world. The banker's world which we have made or by which we are held prisoners, is a monstrosity, a disease, a product of sin. In that world all things are made for sale. Labour itself (and that it to say, Prayer; for to labour is to pray) is a commodity to be bought and sold. In such a world we may offer ourselves as burnt offerings, but we cannot offer praises, we cannot praise God in our works.

What is a work of art? A word made flesh. That is the truth, in the clearest sense of the text. A word, that which emanates from mind. Made flesh; a thing, a thing seen, a thing known, the immeasurable translated into terms of the measurable. From the highest to the lowest that is the substance of works of art. And it is a rhetorical activity; for whether by the ministry of angels or of saints or by the ministry of common workmen, gravers or gravediggers, we are all led heavenwards.

CHAPTER XV

WORK

As USUAL it is necessary to begin at the beginning. Work, as the dictionary says, is "the exertion of energy, physical or mental." In common speech, however, we distinguish between the exertion of energy for the sake of pleasure or recreation, and the same exertion when it is made for the sake of or as a means to the earning or procuring of the means of living. The former we commonly call play; the word work we commonly reserve for those occupations by means of which we get food, clothing, and shelter—the necessaries of life.

It is clear, therefore, that work is a good thing, for that which enables us to live must be good. We must assume that to live is good and that therefore to work is good. And we may freely agree with the Apostle when he says: "if any man will not work neither let him eat," for to eat what the labour of others has produced is, unless freely given, a form of robbery and, as the same Apostle says elsewhere: "he that stole, let him now steal no more; but rather let him labour, working with his hands the thing which is good. . . ."

God has made the world and he has made man such that labour, that is to say, work, is necessary for life, and God cannot have made necessary that which in itself is bad. Moreover, as Solomon, inspired by the Holy Spirit, said: ". . . nothing is better than for a man to rejoice in his work, and this is his portion."

Now it follows from these things that nothing which truly subserves our life can be bad, and therefore there can be no form of necessary work which is in itself degrading. In these latter days we have to be more than usually clear in our minds about this. The idea is prevalent that physical labour is a bad thing, a thing to be avoided, a thing from which we may rightly seek release. We cannot discuss the question of work, the question of the factory system, of the machine, of the arts, until we have right notions as to the nature of physical labour itself. For there can be nothing made, either for man's service or for his pleasure, which is not, at bottom, dependent upon some amount of physical labour for its existence. Even in the most highly organized industrial world, with all the necessaries of life made by machines minded by machines, there will have to be at least the makers of machines and the machine overseers, and there will have to be designers of machines and designers of machine products. Further, there will have to be all the army of officials and administrators, and all the doctors, lawyers, and school teachers, and all these professional persons will be dependent upon a subordinate army of clerks and typists. Then there will be the transport workers of all kinds, and in all these occupations there will be a basis of actual physical labour. So the question remains as before: is physical labour good or bad? Is it a thing to be reduced to a minimum because it is in itself a bad thing, unworthy of "the mystical mug called man," or is it in itself a good thing and only bad when it is done under bad conditions, conditions physically or hygienically unhealthy or morally bad, or when the product is inferior or unsuitable for human use?

Now, as we have seen, according to Christian doctrine, physical labour is not in itself bad, but, on the contrary, because it is necessary for the preservation and continuance of human life, it is in itself good and may be and should be holy and sacred. We have to start with this doctrine. At every turn our object must be to sanctify rather than to exclude physical labour, to honour it rather than to degrade it, to discover how to make it pleasant rather than onerous, a source of pride rather than of shame. And we have to begin by realizing that, in itself and in a christian society, there is no kind of physical labour, no kind whatsoever, none, which is either derogatory to human beings or incapable of being sanctified and ennobled. There is no kind of physical labour which is at one and the same time truly necessary to human life and necessarily either unduly onerous or unpleasant. This is the first thing to grasp, and it is perhaps the most difficult to-day. For considering the conditions of industrialized life in Europe and America, and according to the special kind of town mind which industrialism has begot and fostered (if we may thus, though unwillingly, ennoble a mechanism by speaking of it in such terms), there is nothing to be said about physical labour except that it is to be avoided as much as possible.

In sports and pastimes physical exertion is delighted in, but in the things we do to earn our living we regard the elimination of physical exertion as desirable in itself and a mark of good civilization. We regard physical labour as barbarous. We regard the sight of hundreds of men and girls doing simple repetitive operations requiring the minimum of strength and the minimum of intelligence as a sign of advancement from the primitive life of savages to the full stature of man made in God's image.

We are not concerned in this article to discuss the historical causes of our industrialism, its origin in the greed of manufacturers and merchants and its development under the sway of banks and financiers. The one and only point here is the nature of work in itself, and our object is to rebut the common belief, which industrialism must necessarily encourage, that, as an eminent Catholic writer has recently said: *"such manual work is, of itself, subhuman drudgery."* This is not only untrue but subversive of the whole Christian doctrine of man. Unfortunately, in the circumstances of our industrial world, nothing could seem more obvious common sense. When we consider the working life of the millions of factory-hands, of shop assistants and clerks, of transport workers, and of the agricultural labourers on our de-

124

graded farms, it is obvious that much of the work is, indeed, sub-human drudgery and it cannot but seem a good thing that, by the use of machinery, at least the physical pain has been elim-inated. So it has come about that we have come to believe that physical labour is in itself bad. We seek to reduce it to a mini-mum, and we look to our leisure time for all enjoyable exercise of our human bodies. We do not notice the contradiction. For if physical labour is a thing rightly to be eliminated from work be-cause it is derogatory then it should rightly be eliminated from play also, which is absurd.

It should be obvious that it is not physical labour which is bad, but the proletarianism by which men and women have be-come simply "hands," simply instruments for the making of money by those who own the means of production, distribution, and ex-change. And those who argue in favour of the still further elimi-nation of physical labour on the ground that much manual work is, of itself, subhuman drudgery are either playing into the hands of those for whose profit the mechanical organization of industry has been developed, or they are playing into the hands of the communists and others who look to the Leisure State as the *summum bonum*.

We must return again and again to the simple doctrine: physical labour, manual work, is *not* in itself bad. It is the neces-sary basis of all human production and, in the most strict sense of the words, physical labour directed to the production of things needed for human life is both honourable and holy. And we must remember that there are no exceptions. It is frequently said in extenuation of industrialism that, for instance, modern sanitary engineering has not only lessened the danger of disease, but has done away with much unpleasant and degrading labour in the disposal of sewage. It is said that with sawing and lifting machin-ery we have done away with the unduly arduous; that with the power-loom we have done away with the slave labour of the old weavers. And in the domestic world we claim to have released the housewife and the mother from many or all of those labours known as "domestic drudgery," thus setting her free for "higher things." In all these cases we forget that we had, first of all, by the conditions of town life or commercial exploitation so degraded these various kinds of labour that they were no longer capable of being viewed as pleasant and still less as sacred. And having thus degraded labour, making men and women into mere "hands" and beasts of burden, instruments of profit-making, having allowed, and even encouraged, the growth of the monstrous conglomerations we still call towns and cities, we turn round and curse the very idea of labour. To use the body, our arms and legs and backs, is now held to be derogatory to our human dignity. This then, is the first thing, and it is at the very base of the christian reform for which we stand, that we return to the honouring of bodily labour.

We have said nothing about the spiritual and creative and personal side of human work. Greatly as we have dishonoured and corrupted and destroyed the arts and crafts of men, reducing the workman to a "subhuman condition of intellectual irresponsibility," the root of the matter is in the dishonouring of physical work, and until we have eradicated the prevailing notion that some kinds of work are, of their nature, subhuman drudgery, all discussion of human labour is futile.

But it is relevant to note that in what are generally agreed to be the "highest" forms of human production, "the fine arts," those of painting and sculpture, for example, physical labour is still honoured. In spite of the tendency in recent centuries for sculptors to relegate the actual job of stone-carving to hired labourers (and among painters the grinding of pigments and the preparing of the material to be painted on is now generally done in factories by machinery) nevertheless, it is still recognized that if the thing to be made is to be as good as it can be, the artist himself must use his own hands to do the work. With regard to this the supporters of industrialism say, of course, that in the fine arts the thing made depends for its quality upon the actual personality of its maker, while in ordinary objects of human use this is not so. But apart from the fact that in a normal society "the artist is not a special kind of man, but every man is a special kind of artist," and that, therefore, there is no such hard distinction between the fine arts and others, the point here is this: "that certain kinds of work which, in other circumstances, we regard as drudgery, which could be done by machinery if we so chose, are not so done. In fact, when the nature of the work demands it we willingly endure what our mechanistically-minded reformers find derogatory to human dignity and even delight in it and honour it, and it is only dullness of mind and lack of imagination which prevents the said reformers from seeing that *all* things made could be, and should be, regarded as we regard the products of artists."

It is impossible in a short article to show how these contentions apply throughout the whole world of labour. We can but repeat that in all those cases where it seems that mechanization has brought release from "sub-human drudgery," the drudgery is not inherent in the nature of the work, "of itself," but in the sub-human conditions consequent upon commercialism, industrialism, and the abnormal growth of cities. Whether or no we continue the present mechanistic trend or decide to deliberately restrict machinery (though the possibility of so doing is doubtful) depends ultimately upon the line we take with regard to the ownership of land and work-shops. In a later article we shall see how the ownership of property is the chief means to the resuscitation of the dignity of physical labour and also of the quality of things made.

CHAPTER XVI

PRIVATE PROPERTY

"The exercise of art or work is the formal reason of individual appropriation; but only because it presupposes the rational nature and personality of the artist or workman.

"In the case of the bee . . . there is no exercise of art or of work in the strict sense (since there is no reason in operation); neither is there any individual ownership."

MARITAIN, *Freedom in the Modern World*

"Every man has by nature the right to possess private property as his own.

"As many as possible of the people should be induced to become owners.

"That which is required to preserve life is produced from the soil, but not until man has brought it into cultivation and expended upon it his solicitude and skill. By such act he makes his own that portion of nature's field which he cultivates . . . on which he leaves the imprint of his individuality.

"How must one's possessions be used? Man should not consider his material possessions as his own but as common to all, so as to share them without hesitation when others are in need."

LEO XIII, *Rerum Novarum*

At the very root of all our arguments for the institution of property is the fact that man is a person, and he requires, therefore, not merely food, clothing, and shelter as such, but that particular food, clothing, and shelter which is conformed to his unique personality. And parallel, as it were, with that fact is the fact that the material world into which he is born is such that only by his personal deliberate manipulation can material be made conformable to his needs.

There is only one necessary thing which is obtainable without deliberate labour, the air we breathe; all other necessities are in one degree or another the product of labour. If men were not persons, possessing proprietary right over themselves, mastery over themselves and over their acts, it would be possible to feed, clothe, and house them in herds and regiments and hives, and the claim to personal and private ownership of the means of production would have no rational ground. The present inclination to live in large conglomerations of identical apartments and the mass-production of food, clothing, furniture, building materials, and even houses indicates a widespread degradation of personality. The communist and other political systems which postulate the abolition of private property are products of the same degradation, and all alike are the consequence of the decay of personal ownership which industrialism has caused. For though the owners of industrial enterprises are given to boasting their close attachment to the institution of property, the effect of their politics has been the proletarianization of the masses of workers, and in the minds of the majority of persons to-day the idea of property is not ownership of the means of production, but simply ownership of a share of the money profits of industry and of the mass-produced furniture and pleasure-things (cars, wireless sets, etc.) which money can buy.

Now, physical and mental labour upon the earth and upon raw materials is the primary necessity for the preservation of human life. We may now go farther and we may say that as the object of human life is man's sanctification, labour being the means of life is the appointed means to holiness and thus to beatitude. It should be clear, therefore, that of all kinds of ownership, that of the means of production is the most important, and so important is it that, as Pope Leo XIII says, it is a natural right, natural, that is to say, in accord with the will of God; it is God's will for man. We have, therefore, two things to bear in mind: the necessity of labour, and the consequent natural right to property. The one follows from the other; for it is man, a person, who must labour and "the very essence of this activity is to imprint on matter the mark of rational being." (Maritain, *loc. cit.*)

The root principles of private property being thus understood, we have next to consider the conditions of ownership in our society, and then we should consider possible remedies for the ills we discover. It is, of course, true that there are many ways in which property is held to-day in England, and it is held by many different classes of persons; but it is also true to say that the thing we call proletarianism is the special and peculiar mark of our time. A proletarian is one who owns nothing but his power to labour and that of his children; children are his only "real property." At all times and in all countries there have been proletarians, but in no previous society has the propertyless man been politically free! The Roman or American slave was by law *incapable* of owning anything; the industrial slave is only debarred by the economic circumstances in which the owners of industrial property have deliberately contrived to place him; for it was to the great advantage of industrialists that there should be large numbers of men economically powerless. Cheap labour was essential to them, and no labour is so cheap as that of men who own nothing but their bodily strength.

But as man has a natural right to property, so he has a natural necessity to live in social collaboration with his fellow men. "The State is bound to protect natural rights. . . . If it forbids its citizens to form associations it contradicts the very principle of its own existence. . . ." (Leo XIII, *loc. cit.*) Therefore, in spite of the desperate opposition of owners of land and factories, the Trades Unions, after much bloody and cruel proscription, established themselves and were able to force upon the owners better conditions of labour and better pay. But the result was that a very great impetus was given to the development of machinery. The inventive ingenuity of men has always been available, but never before was it thus used for the exclusive service of men whose main concern was not the improvement of things made, still less the convenience of the workers, but primarily the monetary aggrandisement of themselves. The rising cost of human labour which Trades Unionism brought about made it necesasry, from the point of view of those whose main concern was (and is) profits, to seek every possible means of substitution. Thus, first of all men were enslaved by proletarianization, then they were degraded by factory employment ("for from the factory dead matter goes out improved whereas men there are corrupted and degraded" (*Pius XI, Quad. Anno*) and, as the present Pope has said: "in this age of mechanization the human person becomes merely a more perfect tool in industrial production and a perfected tool for mechanized warfare"); and lastly, they are, as far as possible, deprived of occupation altogether. That is the logical culmination of the mechanization of industry, whether under capitalism or any other form of society, for the main object of machinery is the elimination of human labour.

Now it is clear that no remedy is possible unless, in the first place, we desire it, and, particularly, unless those who use and mind machines desire it; and in the second place, unless those who desire a remedy have the necessary power to effect it. As to the first thing, in order to inculcate a desire for a remedy we must, impossible though it sounds, difficult though it be, regain in ourselves a true conception of the nature of man and of the nature of human work, and we must succeed in converting our fellow men and women. In this endeavour we should be assisted by the growing misery of our times and the palpable breakdown of the materialist society in which we live. But this misery and that breakdown will not be sufficient in themselves; for there are other diagnoses of our disease besides the christian one, and unless we are prepared and active a fascist or communist remedy will be applied, and neither the subordination of man to the State which is essential to the fascist theory nor the materialist interpretation of history which is essential to modern communism is compatible with christian doctrine.

That is the first thing, the reconversion of England to Christianity and to Christ. But in respect of the matter which we are specially concerned in this article, the conversion of England will not suffice unless we understand that this implies much more than Sunday attendance and obedience to the Commandments of the Church. It implies also a clear knowledge of the essentials of a christion society and a determination to recreate it.

In addition to desiring a remedy we must know what the remedy is and understand its nature. The ill from which we are suffering is the decay of personality. The remedy is the revival of personal property. Under industrialism the majority of the people are deprived of personal control of their work, and such control is impossible without ownership. What you do not own you cannot control. What you do not control you are not responsible for. If you are not responsible you cannot be either praised or blamed. Christian doctrine lays it down as a first principle that man has free will and is, therefore, a responsible person— master of his acts and the intended consequences of his acts. This doctrine is flouted and denied in our society. In all but name England is a servile state.

The irresponsibility of the workman is the first and simplest way in which to see our evil condition. It is the first because the exercise of work is the formal reason of individual appropriation. It is the simplest because the exercise of work is within the experience of all but a small class of persons. But though it is the first reason the exercise of work is not the only reason of personal and private ownership. The second, and depending on the first, is the security and dignity of the family. The proletarian is insecure, that is his first misery. He lives in perpetual fear. Thus, all decency and dignity in human life is destroyed. "They do not know that they have renounced normal and natural responsibilities which even savages enjoy, they do not own their homes, their tools or the choice of trade; the power to bring up children, and the means to keep their aged and infirm have been surrendered to a malignant bureaucracy . . . from revolution they hope to gain not more responsibility, but (simply) a greater hold on the pipe line supposed to exist between ourselves and plenty." Therefore it is that Pope Leo says: "The right to property must belong to a man in his capacity of head of a family." Thus and thus alone can the principle of responsibility be brought to bear not merely upon the works of our hands (which, in any case, will be "as straw" on the last day) but upon the fruit of our loins.

But ultimately the most important fruit of individual appropriation, of private property, is the exercise of charity. We are responsible persons, responsible for what we do and for what we make. To what end is this doing and making? The greatest happiness of the greatest number, says the politician (forgetting for the moment that he lives under the shadow of the Whip); my own greatest happiness and enjoyment, says the individual (forgetting altogether that he is "standing in a perpetual queue waiting for a dole which is dependent for its coming on distant workers and an elaborate system of transport"); "that he may have something to give to him that suffers need," says the apostle; "to share them without hesitation," adds the Pope.

"Something to give"—that is the primary thought and the last word. In the word "give" we have the key to the whole problem. Whether it be the workman who must give himself for the good of the work to be done, or the parents who must provide for their children, or all of us who must live in love and charity with our neighbours, in every case economic freedom is necessary to support and make materially effective the precepts of the Gospel. Only upon this basis can a christian society be built—a christian society, that is to say, a society of free men united in and by the love of Christ—free men, that is to say, men who enjoy the ownership of land and workshops, who own not merely themselves but the means of production. For you cannot give what is another's. You cannot give yourself if you are a slave. A proletarian cannot even provide for the *proles* from whom he derives his name. Organized state "charity" is no substitute for the love of our neighbours. "Faith without works is dead," but our works cannot be good works unless they are our own.

The discussion of the political means which must be employed to give effect to the demand for property and responsibility (should we succeed in reviving it) is not within the scope of this article. In any case, the revival of workers' ownership, if it is to be a real, personal ownership and not a mere state capitalism, or bureaucratic socialism, must be gradual, as gradual, indeed, as the spread of a desire for it. At the present time there is hardly any desire for responsibility and, at the most, the only desire for ownership is a desire for an equitable share of industrial profits, for more money, shorter hours, more amusement, and fewer babies. Among all classes, among the poor no less than the rich, the quantitative advantages of industrialism are held to outweigh all its evils, and they cling desperately to the hope that the evils can be removed without loss of the pleasures and conveniences. In these circumstances ownership is still the first necessity. It is futile to preach the christian doctrine of responsibility to people who, by the nature and conditions of their work, can have none. "As many as possible of the people should be induced to become owners," that is all that can be said at present—induced, persuaded, encouraged, helped—with this qualification: that it be understood that ownership means control and responsibility and not merely a share of the profits. An immediate return to small workshops is impossible; the first step must be that the workers gain, in whole or in part, a real ownership of existing industrial enterprises—the workers, those who do the work, of whatever grade, and not the anonymous and irresponsible investors of money.

CHAPTER XVII

EDUCATION FOR WHAT?

WHAT is the general object and end of Education?

Obviously, you cannot lead a person in a way unnatural to him. When you teach, bring up, train a horse, it is always remembered that it is a horse you are dealing with. We do not try anything else. But with human beings we are much more muddled. It seems as though we hardly know what human beings are or what they are for. Yet, obviously, that is the first thing to find out. What is a human being? What end is he made for?

In the world to-day, whatever we say about it, we act almost entirely as though human beings had no reason for being except to *get on* in the world—to acquire a lot of material possessions— to get a good paying job. That seems to be considered the first and most important thing. On top of that we think it would be a good thing if people had a sort of ornamental veneer of culture and good manners—that they be able to appreciate good books and to speak with a refined accent.

This ambition of parents to give children such an education as will enable them to *get on* and get *a good job* is obviously due to a certain view of what a human being is. Whatever we may *say*, we *act* as though a human being was simply a creature, an animal, whose sole job it was to earn his living, acquire ample means to live comfortably, and then pass out. This seems to be the sole object of existence of other animals, and we seem to think that man is only an animal among animals. The only difference between man and other animals seems to be that whereas other animals reproduce their kind to the utmost of their powers and without consideration of their *own* comfort or convenience, men and women, on the other hand, though they have as strong an instinct for mating as other animals, do not proceed in this matter unselfishly or without regard to their own comfort and convenience. And so we find that the more successful we are in the pursuit of riches, the more we *get on* and get rich, so much the more we think of our comfort and so much the more we restrict our families. Perhaps other animals would do the same if they had more wits. But they do not, and so it seems that the main difference between man and other animals is that men are cleverer and more cunning and more self-regarding and *more selfish,* and that our desire for culture and good manners is bound up with *getting on;* for the better your manners, the more likely you are to beat your more boorish competitors, and the more proofs you can show of having learnt poetry and foreign languages, so much the more will you outshine your fellows.

So it seems that to-day our definition of man is: That he is an animal who exists in order to enjoy himself while he lives, and therefore the object of education is to draw out all those faculties which are suitable to that end. First of all, he must learn how to acquire a good living, and, secondly, how to enjoy it in the manner least likely to endanger it. We must learn how to acquire riches and we must learn not to squander them in riotous living. Shorn of all camouflage, that represents the general line of people's ideas to-day. That is not what we *say,* but it is how we *act.* And even the more *highbrow* people are really acting in the same way; for though, perhaps, they say that the object of education is to draw out the very best that is in us—to teach us to know ourselves and control ourselves so that we may enjoy ourselves even more—it all comes to the same thing—to acquire the means to live well and then to enjoy life. For, after all, the saying, "Eat, drink and be merry," depends upon its interpretation. It does not necessarily mean eat and drink as much as possible, but eat and drink as much as will enable you to be merry. And being merry does not necessarily mean buffoonery and horseplay and drunken revelry; it may mean the most refined high-art enjoyments. So whether we are *highbrows* or *lowbrows*, the definition of man which is accepted to-day comes to the same thing: in either case it means that we have no idea of man except that his only reason for existence is to get on in this world and have as good a time as possible.

Perhaps there are two chief causes of this rather limited view of man:

(1) The decay and disappearance of unity in religion; and

(2) The tremendous growth of the power and prestige of the commercial world.

But perhaps these two things are two sides of the same thing; for where religion is strong, commerce is always weak. So perhaps we may say that the one and only cause of our limited and materialistic view of man is the decay of religious unity, for where there are a hundred rival sects there cannot be power. The devil may well approve of the military rule, *Divide and conquer.* For where, instead of one religion swaying the hearts and minds of men, there are a hundred rival religions, it is obvious that no one of them can be really powerful, and no one of them can unite us all together and inspire us.

There is no need for me to say here which, if any, of the rival religions is, in my opinion, the true one. I am only pointing out that, in the absence of religious unity, the one and only thing which can unite men is the desire of material riches. Religion, they now say, is your private affair—nothing to do with how the state is run—nothing to do with how you earn your living— nothing to do with your work.

But if the common materialistic view of man leaves much to be desired—and few people are really satisfied with it—it is obviously a very limited view and takes no account of those qualities in men which we all agree to admire most: humility, unselfishness, tenderness, except in so far as they help us to *get on*—and it takes no account of the quite common appetite of men for something real and unchanging and not liable to decay and death—I say, if the common materialistic definition of man leaves much to be desired, what other view is there? If man is not just an animal among animals, what is he? Well, I think, even without entering into the awful field of religious controversy, we may say certain things. God exists; He is a Person—the Personal Author and Ruler of all things. And *we are His people and the sheep of His pasture*. And we are made in His image—that is to say, we share in God's spiritual nature. We are rational beings and can deliberate and weigh the pros and cons of action; and having thus weighed, we can act freely. Whether or no we can do good of ourselves, we can certainly refrain from evil, even if we are to some extent—perhaps to a large extent—the victims of our physical and psychological *make-up*. We are, therefore, rightly held to be *responsible persons* and not automata obeying willy-nilly the forces to which we find ourselves subjected. And if we are thus children of God—for we are, in this religious view of man, more than just animals without responsibility (after all, you can punish a dog—but you cannot really *blame* him)—if we are children of God, then we are heirs also. We are called to some sort of sharing with God in His own life. We have what we call a *vocation*. We have, in fact, a destiny independent of our physical life on this earth. A destiny for which this physical life is a training ground and place of preparation. It is, in fact, a school—a place where we are *educated*.

It is clear then, is it not? that if we accept the religious view of man's nature, we are compelled to take a very different, a radically different view of education. No longer can we think merely of *getting on* in the commercial and materialistic sense. We must now think of getting on in the sense of getting heavenwards. And in everything we learn and in everything we teach to our children or our pupils, we must bear this fact in mind. We must learn to get on in the world—not as an end in itself, but as a means to getting heavenwards. Any education which neglects this fact, and to the extent to which it neglects it, is false education, because it is false to man. It is untrue; it is not in accordance with his nature as child of God and heir also.

All this sounds very pious—though there is no harm in that—and some people will think that I am advocating an almost total neglect of practical things—that perhaps I despise worldly success, that I despise reading, writing, and arithmetic and dancing and gymnastics and science and history. That is not so. What I am saying is simply that as parents and teachers we must teach these things with *an eye on our goal*. If, like the materialists, and that is, in practice, most people to-day, we think there is *no* goal, then of course, there is nothing to be said against that kind of education which has for its sole object the training of children to win prizes and get good jobs, and we should then approve of the London County Council which says in its advertisements of its evening classes:

Turn your energy into pounds, shillings, and pence.
L.C.C. Evening Classes offer a good return on your investment.

and we should approve of our men of business, who see everything in terms of money—who think that the production of dividends is the first object of industrial enterprise (as the Railway Stockholders' Union says: *British Railways are in business to earn dividends*); for to the man of business, the only criterion of what is good is what will sell.

But if we do not accept the materialist philosophy, if we do not agree with the economic interpretation of history, if we do not think man is nothing more than a creature made for gaining material wealth, if we take the religious point of view—because, if we think for half a moment, we know that we are not satisfied with working merely to make money to buy things which have been made by people who only made them in order to sell them . . . then we shall take a radically different view of education.

We shall even take a radically different view of arithmetic and of reading and writing—because we shall attack them in a totally different frame of mind. That is the point. It is not that we shall do nothing but write hymns, though the best poems are hymns. It is not that we shall only read the Bible, though the Bible is the best book, or that we shall only count how much we can give away (instead of counting how much we can spend), it is simply that we shall see all things as in some way heavenly or leading heavenwards. For education will not then mean drawing out those faculties which make us successful worldlings, but drawing out those faculties which make us better fitted for an eternal rather than a merely temporary existence. We shall see everything, as the philosopher says, *sub specie æternitatis*—that is to say we shall see everything *in its real shape,* its eternal shape, the shape of its *being* rather than the shape of its *doing.* For it is not what we *do* that matters most, but what we *are.* And it is the same with things as with persons. Being is more important than doing. But if, like the materialists and their followers, the business men of to-day, we say there is no being behind doing, but only doing, then we shall not only lose the Kingdom of God in heaven but also the Kingdom of God on earth. Newport and Swansea, Birmingham and the Black Country, Manchester, Glasgow, the wilds of east and south-east London! What could be more ungodly? And what could more plainly be the proper reward of our greed and avarice and our refusal to educate ourselves and our children except to *get on* or *get out?* And the *war, pestilence, and famine,* which are upon us, what are they but the due reward of our sins?

But in spite of our enthusiasm for worldly success, we all know that a worldly view of education is very unsatisfactory—to say the least. It does not satisfy us. We want something more. And very often we think that all will be well if, in addition to learning things which will be useful to enable us to *get on,* we add what we call *cultured subjects*—a spot of *art,* a spot of poetry and foreign languages, just in the same way as people build banks and town halls with iron frames and concrete and all the cheapest and most labour-saving methods, and then cover the front with elaborate stonework in imitation of a classical temple, with columns and carvings.

So we think that children should have a *good, sound practical education,* which will enable them to make money—that is the iron and concrete part—and that then they should have culture— that is the pillars and carvings on the front. We all know those buildings (they are everywhere), which have fine imitation Queen Anne or Gothic or Classic fronts and then when you go into the backyard you see only white glazed bricks and drain pipes—as someone said: *Queen Anne fronts and Mary Anne backs.* But we can easily see that this is all nonsense; for if we cannot make our buildings fine and noble and beautiful all through, front and back and inside and out, then it would be much better, more honest and more holy, to confine ourselves to the Mary Anne part alone, and see how truly well and nobly we can do the drains and the drain-pipes, and leave out the sham architecture.

And so it is with education. If we cannot give our children a truly religious education, through and through, so that everything they learn is in harmony with their ultimate heavenly destiny, then it would be much better if we confined ourselves to the plain bread-and-butter part of the business and simply taught them practical things—the three R's and physical jerks and how to read a Bradshaw and drive a car—and leave out the classics and Shakespeare and all the sham culture.

For culture is a sham if it is only a sort of Gothic front put on an iron building—like the Tower Bridge—or a classical front put on a steel frame—like the *Daily Telegraph* building in Fleet Street. Culture, if it is to be a real thing and a holy thing, must be the product of what we actually do for a living—not something added, like sugar on a pill.

So it all comes back to this: What is man? Is he just an animal for whom earthly life is all? Or is he a Child of God with eternal life in view?

141

CHAPTER XVIII

PEACE AND POVERTY

"We desire peace—but not the things that make for peace."

WE WANT food—but not an agricultural England. We prefer to buy foreign food from joint stock companies whose only concern is dividends.

We want clothing and shelter—but not craftsmen to make them. We prefer machines and dividends.

We want amusement—but do not want to amuse ourselves. We prefer the cinema to the theatre, and the wireless and "pools" —and more money. And what do we want money for? To buy things, of course—and we forget that we can only buy things which have been made by people who only made them to sell them. We work in order to get money to buy things which have been made by people who only made them to get money. We think we want money to buy good things (goods), but we forget that there are no good things to buy, because when things are only made to sell, the standard is not goodness but saleability.

So we want peace—but "not the things that make for peace." We have set our minds on riches. Men of commerce and financiers rule our world.

For the plain truth is: only in poverty can we have peace— and "he that loseth his life shall save it."

He has put down the mighty from their seat, and raised up the humble.

"He has filled the hungry with good things, and the rich He has sent away empty." (Song of Mary.)

It is absolutely essential that we should grasp this fact, this truth: Until we have done so and, more, until we have learnt to act upon it, peace is impossible—unattainable.

They say: If you want peace, prepare for war, but this is proven nonsense. If you want peace, you must prepare for peace.

And the first preparation for peace is the preparation of the mind. And the first preparation of the mind is the acceptance of poverty.

But, need it be said? by poverty is meant a good thing—not a bad.

Poverty, chastity, obedience!

When we speak of chastity, we do not mean something evil. We do not mean the evil chastity, the enforced chastity of young people who would but cannot marry (the banks will not let them). . . .[1]

When we speak of obedience, we do not mean something evil. We do not mean the evil obedience of slaves—the servile obedience of factory hands ("coolies")—men reduced to a sub-human condition of intellectual irresponsibility—whose only responsibility is to do what they are told—who are only fully human when they are not working—whose only reason for working is the pay they get for doing it—whose only reason for obedience is fear of the "sack."

So when we speak of poverty, we do not mean evil poverty—destitution, penury, nakedness, starvation, homelessness—the evil poverty of those who are deprived of the just necessities of living, whose one thought is to get food and warmth, and when fed and warmed, to sleep. When we speak of poverty, we mean a good thing, a holy thing like that chastity—a holy thing, the fruit of

[1] Some banks forbid their employees to marry until they are earning a certain salary—a salary not usually received by men under about thirty to thirty-five years of age.

reason—like that obedience, also a holy thing, the fruit of love, the love of God—"whose service is perfect freedom." So poverty is lovely and beloved—"Blessed are the poor in spirit for theirs is the Kingdom of Heaven."

.   .   .   .   .   .

But let us come down to earth—brass tacks. And let us say, with the theologian, that "poverty is the rational attitude towards material things"—the only rational attitude in a material world.

But poverty begins in the mind—it is first of all a way of believing, thinking, feeling—it is a way of the spirit. And it is precisely the opposite way to "the way of the world"—our world, the world of England, of Empire, the way of France, America, the way of Communism, which seeks to make the poor rich—but Christ came to make the rich poor and the poor *holy*.

Do you not see that the whole world is set on riches—on money making and the increase of material things? It is our one idea of advancement—more things, more food, more clothes, more rooms in our houses, more speed, more comfort, more luxury, more amusements, and, to get all these things, more money, more dividends—more colonial supplies of "raw materials," more "spheres of influence," more trading agreements.

War began, in the dim light of prehistory, with robbery—the perfectly natural and innocent propensity of animals to obtain food and possessions by force. But man, whatever we guess about his origins, has always been impeded by conscience—sense of good and evil, by reason, a sense of right and wrong, true and false, and by law, the "natural" law, the law of God. He has always imposed law on himself—or had law imposed on him. "Thou shalt not steal—thou shalt not kill. . . ." Such things are not only wicked but unreasonable—not only crime but folly, not only sin but silly.

But not until about two thousand years ago—with Confucius, with Buddha, with Christ . . . did men see, as it were suddenly, that law could be transcended, that men could do good because they willed good and not merely because they were prevented from doing evil.

This is the revelation that religion has made. Religion means "rule" and the rule is that "the service of God is perfect freedom." And the service of God means poverty.

Imagine the opposite! Thou shalt seek riches and despise the poor. . . . Thou shalt bend all thy energies to the accumulation of possessions. Give nothing away—rather take away from others. If your neighbour's trade is prosperous undersell him and take his trade away from him. Buy cheap and sell dear. Hoard your stocks of goods, in the hope that scarcity will force your neighbours to pay higher prices. Take no thought for the quality of the goods you make or of the services you render—think only whether they be saleable. Give nothing for nothing, and as little as possible for sixpence. Value everything in pounds, shillings, and pence, otherwise you may be tempted to think of quality rather than quantity. Make everything as cheaply as possible, and in mass, so that you may tap the largest markets. Pay your labourers the least they will take. Remember that your duty is to your shareholders, otherwise they will not invest their capital. Make your bankers and financiers and men of business your rulers— what you want is a business government. Make your princes into puppets and your priests into recruiting sergeants for your armies.

For the rich man must be armed that his possessions may be defended and increased, and how should poor men be persuaded to fight for him unless it be made to seem that they fight for honour and justice?

Such are the necessary prescriptions in a world determined to pursue riches. Only thus can riches be won—only thus can riches be defended. The pursuit of riches is the beginning of war and war is the necessary, inevitable, right and proper and logical accompaniment of that pursuit.

And as the pursuit of riches is the natural propensity of animals, so animals are naturally fighters. The country farmyard is full of savage beasts—the quiet hedgerow is full of vegetables armed to the teeth. Hence, as men refuse the teaching of Christ—which would redeem them from their fall into animalism—so they take naturally to war. When you think of the horrors of the shambles which war is—to-day no less and even more than in the past—it becomes clear that unless war be in some way "natural," no one would willingly endure it.

But nothing is more "natural." Hence not only priests, but women, rejoice in it. Women are even better in efficiency than priests as recruiting sergeants.

For women are, in the nature of things, more worldly, less childish than men. Women desire possessions, riches, even more wholeheartedly than men, with an even deeper tenacity.

This is inevitable—their children and their children's advancement, their homes and the support of their homes; honour, worldly success, worldly honour, respectability, all these things are as the breath of life to mothers of children. Hence the amazing readiness of women to urge men to war. This war, here and now, may mean the loss of husband, of sons—and as things are in modern war, it may even mean their own death and the death of their young children—but the deep, hell deep, instinct is not destroyed. Men have fought for possessions, possessions for the home, since the beginning. Two thousand years of Christianity is as nothing to the many thousands of years of man's life on this earth.

Poverty! How should women desire poverty? How indeed should they desire peace? Peace and Poverty!

Do men desire peace? Yes, because war no longer means fighting worthy of the name. But do they desire the things that make for peace? There is not the slightest sign of it. They want a contradiction. They want peace in order to make money undisturbed. But that is for ever impossible—it is as impossible an idea as it is in fact.

Do women want peace? Yes, because war has now come *home* to them. It is no longer a matter of a "thin red line of heroes"—it means bombs in the bedroom. . . . But do they want the things that make for peace? I do not see the slighest sign of that either.

"We live in so depraved an age that were a stranger to compare the words of the Gospel with what in fact goes on, he would infer that men are not followers of Christ but His enemies . . . and the worst of it is that they do not know it." (St John Chrysostom, A.D. 375. *Treatise on Compunction and Penance*.)

What then? Is it as though Christ has not died? No, it is simply as though men and women had entirely forgotten.

Let peacemakers remember. Let them above all remember that it is no manner of good preaching peace unless we preach the things that make for peace—that even the love of our fellowmen is no good unless it means giving rather than taking, yielding rather than holding, sharing rather than exclusive possession, confederation rather than sovereignty, use rather than profit. And it means the subordination of the man of business and the dealer and money-lender, both in the world and, even more, in our own hearts.

"Let him that stole steal no more—rather let him labour, working with his hands. . . ."

CHAPTER XIX

ART AND EDUCATION

ABOLISH ART AND TEACH DRAWING

ART in Education in the language of to-day doesn't mean the relationship existing between the human business of making things and the development of the human personality; it means something much more particular. It means the introduction to the school curriculum of a special subject called Art. Just as we have a special time allotted to religious instruction and another to physical jerks, just as we have a time for French and a time for geography, so we have a time for Art, and Art, in this school sense, means not the general business of making things, but learning about the painting and sculptures (not music; for music is another special subject! with its own allotted time) of past and perhaps present "masters" and, under the more or less enthusiastic instruction of someone with a certificate from the Royal College of Art (or other recognized authority), learning how to do painting and sculpture in the approved sense of the words.

Personally, I think this is all complete nonsense. Many other people think so, too; and they are trying to get it altered. But, as far as I can learn, it is "out of the fat into the fire"; for the reformers are not rebelling against the whole stupid conception of art which prevails to-day, and which is the direct product of "the industrial revolution" and "the renaissance," but are moved by an even more narrow conception, and one which is derived from the same sources as the old.

The Renaissance, i.e., the decay and death of the "traditional" arts and the development of individualism in painting, sculpture, music, and architecture, which accompanied the rise of the merchant class out of medieval feudal and religious rule—and the industrial revolution, i.e., the widespread introduction of the factory system and the subsequent use of machinery which marked the general triumph of the merchant class in the eighteenth century and the final degradation and proletarianization of the peasantry—these movements naturally and inevitably (i.e., such was their *nature*) produced the state of affairs with which we are familiar—the divorce of personality from the work of producing the physical necessaries of life (food, clothing, shelter, and furniture), and the exaggerated value consequently placed upon these arts not subject to factory organization or mechanization, picture painting, sculpture, and music. "Art" thus becomes something special—a special subject. It ceased to be true to say that "the artist is not a special kind of man, but every man is a special kind of artist," [1] and the word came to be applied only to the so-called "fine" arts—the arts which primarily serve the mind, but which now are looked upon as primarily serving the senses (and thus sensibility is regarded as of greater importance, both to the "artist" and to his public, than intellectual power).

This, crudely simplified, is the position to-day. And so the problem arises—what about Art in Education? It seems to me two things stand out. First, in view of the fact that our whole civilization is wrong from top to bottom, and past remedy too, then there is no point whatever in merely tinkering with the surface of it, and it is not only no use, it is definitely bad to infect the ordinary people of the middle, professional, and "working" classes with the corrupt ideas of the polite upper classes and the "intelligentsia." The idea of "Art" as understood by these latter being wholly bad (because self-centred and merely aesthetic) ought to be generally

[1] Ananda Coomaraswamy, *The Transformation of Nature in Art*, O.U.P., 1934.

spurned and discouraged and not imposed on school children (though alas! the evil is probably already done). Therefore I say the only thing to be done about Art in Education is to scrap it— leave it out altogether. And let artists, i.e., painters and sculptors and musicians, forget their refinement, and their association with picture dealers and art critics, and join in with the revolutionary workers in the effort to wreck the present society. That's the only sound way of reform. For we don't *want* children to think of art as being only pictures and such. We want them to think of it as the exercise of human skill and imagination in *every* department of human work. We must therefore attempt to abolish the word except in its simple sense as meaning "the well making of what needs making," and we shall never talk of art, but only of the arts.

This brings me to my *second* point. Let me assume that we have abolished Art; but there still remain the several arts of writing, drawing, painting, engraving. . . . These things can be taught. If a bootmaker can make boots (very few can to-day) he can show someone else how to do it. If a bricklayer can lay bricks, there's no reason why he shouldn't teach other people. And, similarly, if you can draw with pencil or graver or brush it would be both kind and just if you would hand on your power to others. And these arts are useful arts. They are, like language itself, means of communication. There are many more things worth communicating than can be done by language. That is, indeed, the primary value of the arts of drawing—that they are another kind of language. Those who cannot draw, even with a pencil, are to that extent handicapped. And it is a communication of ideas first of all, of thinkable things—thinkable, but not therefore literary. And it is not primarily a matter of communicating feelings, even fine feelings, or emotions, even the most stirring. Children should be taught to use a pencil precisely, and, no less precisely, a brush— very few of those whom we call artists to-day can do it. We hear a lot about school children being given a chance to express themselves freely and to develop their imaginations. By all means! But we have no business to stuff it into their innocent minds that it is self-expression that matters. That's only the accident, the inevitable accident and accompaniment of all human work normally accomplished. You haven't got to bother about it or belaud it or make children self-conscious about it. In a normal society self-expression needs curbing rather than belauding. Teaching teachers is the real difficulty. Where can we find teachers of drawing who really know what drawing is and how to draw? Drawing! God knows it's simple enough—making things out of lines—real things of real lines. But that's not what our "art" teachers think or do. I've seen better, far better drawings, as such, done by children of seven or eight than by all the academicians and only rivalled by such extraordinary masters as J. Cocteau or D. Jones of Brockley—and not only better drawings, but more precise and more convincing communications—more convincing and therefore, incidentally, more moving.

So, therefore, I say, for the present, let art education rip. Let the children draw—one hour or less, three days a week. Give them a *subject*—just to keep them on the rails. As for instruction, let it be more moral than intellectual. Tell them to be careful and keep their pencils sharp. Tell them not to smudge. Tell them to put down on paper what they really mean and not to scribble. And let the subject be as difficult as you like. Nothing is too difficult for the innocent. Tell them to draw the Blessed Trinity—the destruction of Pompeii—the Nativity of Jesus—flowers in fairyland (close up)—mother making tea—the baby in the bath. Remember they've generally got plenty of visual imagination even if we have not. And all you've got to do is, in reason, to keep them at it—diligence, no slacking. (But I find them keen enough.) And then, of course, they can paint their drawings and make their own paints —but you needn't insist on it—colour isn't all the ladies think it.

This, again, crudely simplified, is a rough idea of what might be done in schools. But don't call it Art—call it drawing (and painting). Art must be abolished—it must, it must, it must.

CHAPTER XX

FIVE HUNDRED YEARS OF PRINTING

As LONG as the great increase of books and other printed matter was kept within the limits imposed by the hand press it seems probable that the world was well served by the invention of movable types. All who had a reasonable need of books were able to get them, and had it not been for the insubordination of men of business who, taking advantage of the proletarianization of the peasantry, which an insubordinate landlordism had effected, were able, by means of the factory system and the division and subdivision of labour, to turn human beings into machines, it is certain that the "power" press would never have been invented or developed, and the consequent plethora of cheap books and magazines and newspapers and advertisement would never have brought the art and craft of printing and the business or profession of publishing into the disgrace they now so abundantly deserve.

"The artist," said Socrates, "is he who is able to make something useful," and this is as true to-day as it was in the time of the Greeks; but now, as then, it behoves us to consider what use and to whom. And directly you ask such questions it becomes clear that the primary use of the art of printing to-day is to produce profits for those who sell it, and that to the majority of those to whom it is sold its primary use is dope.

But these truths, though clear as daylight, are unperceived by all but a few, and for the simple reason that their disclosure would undermine and eventually wreck the whole giant edifice of commercial printing. In "peace," so called, as in what is still called "war," it is of paramount importance "to render to God what is Caesar's"—to make honour and justice and the service of our fellow men appear the main reasons for our actions. Therefore the real truth about the printing trade goes unnoticed and unannounced, and just as the Lancashire cotton magnates are happy to hide behind the Indian Civil Service and, with that protection, to pretend that they are only interested in India for the good of the Indians, so the rampant commercialism of the printing trade is hidden behind the pretence that the primary object of printers is to supply a hungry world with mental and spiritual pabulum.

In this matter, of course, the printing trade is no different from any other machine industry, and brings on itself the same nemesis. Directly you use any power other than animal power you will, with unfailing necessity, produce more than is needed by the immediate society of the workers. But the printing trade is in this respect worse off than any other, for its market must necessarily be almost completely a home market. The export of English books to non-English speaking countries is as small as that of French or German or other foreign books to England, and the export of English newspapers and advertising matter is equally or even more restricted.

The consequence is that, England being a good fifty years ahead of other nations in Industrialization, Mr Chamberlain was able to export his screws in vast quantities to all parts of the world and, until they industrialized themselves in turn, foreign countries were a profitable market (it's only profits that matter) for British machinery and other British machine products, but the preposterous development of power and speed in printing machinery has only made it more and more urgent that printers should cut one another's throats. And though, from one point of view, it is more desirable that thieves should destroy one another than that they should swamp the unfortunate natives ("after all, the Italians *are* natives, aren't they?") of other countries with the inferior products of machines, this result is not less tragic.

It is probable that the genuine, unstimulated appetite for reading matter was fully satisfied more than a hundred years ago. But commercial competition and the greed of investors could not allow that state of affairs to continue. "Enough is as good as a feast," but not for the chap (b.f. or otherwise) who has more than enough to sell. The first thing to do is to cheapen your costs of production—improve your factory organization, keep wages down. Then, having driven your employees to revolt, you have Trade Unionism and all its inevitable restriction of freedom (for war is war whether in commerce or politics). Then, your "labour" being no longer so physically servile, whatever it may be intellectually, you must, in self defence (though, of course, you will dope yourself with brainy notions of the beauty of machinery and man's God-given powers of ingenuity—"the machine is but the extension of the human hand" and all such tosh), develop machines, or pay investors to do so, and so produce the same amount of printing and eventually, much more at even less cost than before.

In this stage your main trouble, if you are a human person, and even if you are not, will be to get enough work to keep your labour profitably employed (it's only profit that matters). Thus your main function, as an exceedingly eminent university printer said to me, will not be that of a printer but of an employer of labour. But all things pass, and this stage has passed, too. For the aforesaid development of machinery has progressed so rapidly and so prodigiously that what was formerly mainly a labour problem is now a machine problem. The number of workers have been reduced, in proportion to output, beyond all imagined possibility and so, as another eminent printer said to me, the problem is not how to avoid sacking your men but how to keep your machines fed. Thus arrives the advertiser—to advertise printing! An entirely unnatural appetite must be stimulated. It is the last stage of the game. Nothing remains but national dictatorship—or the abandonment of industrialism. I should think dictatorship will win—the investor will thus get a better deal, if he works the thing properly. . . .

I remarked that printers were not able to any very large extent, to sell the inferior product of their machines in foreign countries. This will, of course, seem to be nothing but an entirely unwarranted "rude remark." Perhaps this is the most pathetic aspect of the problem, as it is the most difficult to deal with. In a century and a half of industrialism, with all the forces at their disposal (not forgetting the police and the military), they have very successfully "put it across" that any one who is against their *weltanschauung* must be fool or knave or both. The sacred rights of capital investment must not be insulted, still less hindered.

I imagine nothing can be done about it, except by industrialists themselves, and they are doing very efficiently all that is necessary. Blood and tears are the natural end of anything so inhuman and sub-human as our industrial capitalism and much blood and much tears are now about to be shed. Nevertheless, a word out of season, like Christmas strawberries, may not come amiss. The only difficulty is to know to whom to address it. Printers, on the whole, are jolly pleased with themselves. How can they be otherwise? If you live in and enjoy a world of tubes and buses and Oxford Street architecture and the B.B.C. and the cinema and neon light, and motoring from one ugly place to another (paying sixpence on the way for the privilege of visiting some medieval ruin or a waterfall with barbed wire round it to keep off the penniless), there is no reason whatever why you should not think modern printing much better than anything preceding it.

And we all live in that world, and most of us think it's the best to date; so it's no use presenting my Christmas strawberry to the printers' customers either. How can *they* see anything wrong? As for the other two classes of persons concerned, the investors of capital and the pundits who write up the selling side, the former have no criterion but saleability and the latter, in their enthusiasm to keep their own firm to cut the throats of its rivals, can hardly be expected to cut their own.

But look at your own bookshelves and in your own wastepaper basket! Look at the bookstalls and the posters! Consider the thought that about twenty million newspapers, neither better nor worse than the *Daily Mail* are printed and sold in the British Isles alone every morning! Consider that there are perhaps only ten good books published, i.e., printed, every year—and how many millions of bad ones?—bad to read, bad to look at, and even bad to burn. A great many people admit this—quite freely—but what difference does that make? for, on the one hand, we must keep the machines fed; and on the other, like heroin addicts, forty million people must have their dope.

Five hundred years of printing—what ho! Five million *miles* of printing, five million *tons* of printing, five hundred million bankers' *pounds* of printing, and now five million *men* at one another's throats in order to push the process to its bitter end.

I suppose you think I want to go back to the hand press. Please don't worry. My wants are more modest than that. I only want England to become poor and needy.

CHAPTER XXI

THE LEISURE STATE

THE Leisure State is the grand climax of the industrial world. The two things are obverse and reverse of the same medal; you cannot have one without the other, and you cannot want one and not want the other. The industrial world leads to the Leisure State. The Leisure State is the only possible excuse or palliation of industrialism. If there were no Leisure State looming out of the murky clouds of nineteenth-century industrialism this world would be hell indeed, and every one would agree that it was so. But with the promised land in sight men forget the pains and miseries of the road and the cruelties of the wild beasts besetting it. The haven is near, heaven on earth, the earthly paradise, in which by a reasonable organization of machine facture, transport, and distribution, a reasonable state control of money and credit, "the life blood so to speak of the entire economic body," the great resources of the earth will be available to all, and food, clothing, shelter, and amusement will be as plentiful actually as they are now potentially. Then at last men will be free from the curse of Adam. No more shall it be said "by the sweat of thy brow shalt thou earn bread." No more shall it be true that "he that does not work, neither shall he eat." The lie shall be thrown back in the teeth of Genesis and St Paul. In brief: machinery will have released men for "higher things," and, instead of the weary toil of the slaves of Rome or Egypt, or the no less weary toil of our modern factory slaves, all men, high and low, will be free to spend their long leisure hours in contemplation of the divine mysteries, and in the pursuit of all those fancies and games of which the dark night of primitive and savage labour has deprived the sons and daughters of men. And all this paradise, so longed for, through so many centuries of centuries, will have been the gift of those few men of genius who saw the possibilities of mechanical invention, and of those others who, viewing the world through their telescopes and microscopes, saw it as a giant storehouse of unused and unlimited powers, and had the vision of the rational application of science to industry.

And though these men of genius, scientists, engineers, were supported in the first place by men driven by less worthy motives, the traders and merchants and the successors of traders and merchants, the men of business pure and simple, the money-lenders, and financiers and controllers of credit, nevertheless, we do not need to "scorn the base degrees by which we did ascend," good comes out of evil, and the selfishness and greed and avarice of our first merchants and adventurers, and the even more monstrous greed and avarice of our Victorian and Georgian financiers need not blind us to the blessings which a benign nature had been using them to promote. The young airman throws his bombs on the indefensible slums. The resulting slaughter seems sad and even horrible. But good comes from evil. The Empire is preserved, and justice can again rule the minds of men. So it is in many affairs, and in this matter of the commercial and financial appetites which were the motive power in the first springing and later development of the mechanical and scientific method of production, we may see again the holy triumph of good over evil; we may see the evil appetites as having been instrumental in the conception, birth, childhood, and adolescence of the earthly paradise which is the due and appropriate setting for rational animals; we do indeed "rise on stepping stones of our dead selves to higher things." The commerce- and finance-ridden mind is even now dying; the death-rattle may even now be heard in its abominable throat. Thus we shall emerge and the watchwords of Communism, as indeed of Christianity, "Each for all and all for each," will sound in our hearts without any necessity of a passage through either blood or tears, even tears of repentance—save only that blood and those tears through which we, in our long pilgrimage from our ape-like ancestral home, have already passed.

Science! Machinery! blessed words, and yet more blessed things. All necessary work, as such is understood by Science, shall be done by Machinery, and, it is not too much to predict, the machines themselves shall be minded by machines. Science! Machinery!—and thus Freedom! We have not yet quite arrived; but Science and Mechanics have shown us the way. Nothing remains to be done but to destroy the stronghold of the robbers who have for so long beset our path—and, if possible, convert (why not?) its inmates. The talents which, with so much skill and daring, so much courage and, so to say, self-sacrifice, they have defended themselves, will be of even greater use in the earthly paradise, and will bring them even greater glory among men—the glory of saviours, and the love and devotion of their fellows. As organizers of scientific knowledge and its application to engineering and machine facture they have shown their prowess. It only remains for them to devote such great gifts to the common good instead of their private aggrandizement. Statesmanship has not been wanting among men, and, as in ancient Petra, *rose-red city,* the highway robbers became princes and governors, so let our captains of finance become our honoured leaders and directors.

But, alas! the whole of the foregoing paragraphs is nothing but romantic nonsense. Romantic, that is untrue to the facts of life and of man, untrue to the facts of man's nature, untrue to the nature of the physical world, and to the nature of man's spiritual being. Nonsense, complete nonsense! The world is not like that.

For quite apart from the extreme unlikeliness of any conversion of our commercial and financial over-lords, or even of the millions of small men (ourselves, in fact) to the view that the only true function of machines and of science is the amelioration of man's earthly life and his release from the thraldom of physical labour so that he may spend his time in pure enjoyment and in the contemplation of holy things—quite apart from the fact that the hard-won fruits of our industrialism are more likely to fall from our grasp and the world, our world, go down in the "war, pestilence, and famine" to which the service of riches inevitably tends—quite apart from all that, such a way of life is clean contrary to the nature of this physical world, to man's physical nature, and to the nature of his desires. Moreover, and above all, it is clean contrary to all we know and all that has been revealed as to man's ultimate destiny and Last End. We are not spirits inhabiting, perforce and against our wills, a sort of inanimate motor-cars which we call our bodies, so that the more automatic these cars can be contrived to be, the fuller and richer and more untrammelled will be our spiritual life. We digest our food without any conscious exercise of intelligence and will, and we are glad to be able to do so, and rightly consider ourselves unwell when we do otherwise. But it does not follow that it would be a good thing, therefore, if all the growing and preparation of food, the making and adorning of clothes and houses and town halls and churches, were in like manner reduced to being automatic and unconscious operations, if all the arts of living were reduced to the sphere of the drains. It quite obviously does not follow, and it cannot be made to follow, by any process of logical reasoning even if ordinary people were prepared to accept conclusions so arrived at. It is, on the contrary, quite obvious that not only are all the arts of life—farming and preparing food and eating it, making woven or other fabrics for clothes and furnishings, building all sorts of buildings from the lowliest and most simple sheds and cottages to the most elaborate and ornate palaces and shrines, the whole affair of transport both on land and sea—not only are these occupations the very ones which, for thousands of years, and even now, to-day, in spite of their mechanization, are man's chief means to the enjoyment of life, his chief pride and delight, the things we treasure and which we travel far to see and share—not only this, but they still are, and always have been, the chief means available to him for the expression and manifestation of his spiritual composition. For man is not an angelic and unembodied spirit; his is a composite nature, material and spiritual, both real and both good; and his pleasures are not simply the pleasures of the mind. He is not altogether incapable of such—logic, metaphysics, mathematics, such things enthral some persons no less than the job of building with stone enthrals others. But, such, in general, is not man; and even your mathematician or your monastic ascetic enjoys and promotes the other arts of men; he likes his food and drink; it does not seem inappropriate to him that good wine should adorn his table or that weavers should give as much disinterested love to the fabrics of his clothes as he himself does to his research into the nature of things.

The Leisure State is founded upon a false angelism, a false notion of the fitness of men to enjoy themselves without the direct responsibility of each one to earn his living and that of his wife and children by his own work. This false angelism was, fifteen hundred years ago, called Manicheeism. It is the same illusion to-day. It is the notion that matter is essentially evil and therefore work essentially degrading. No one would express it like that to-day; we do not like such religious-sounding terms. But that is the basis of our Leisure State—the release of man from his entanglement with matter. The highbrow exponents see it in highbrow terms—higher things, high art, beauty, contemplation. . . . Ordinary people are not thus constituted. For them it means simply a release from drudgery and insecurity, from slum-life and overcrowding, from underfed and unhealthy children. It means more travel in motor-cars, at greater speeds, more racing, more football matches; in fact, more of everything but of that dreary business which industrialism has made of work—of which no one could be expected to wish anything but to see the last of it.

And this modern Manicheeism has no foundation in a generous spirituality. It is not the product of an overwhelming love of God, as though one should say with St Paul: "I long to be dissolved and to be with Christ." Far otherwise! Here is no desire for the pure bliss of some beatific vision; here is nothing but a

desire for release from drudgery and privation. Here is no desire
for the time when men will have better food and better drink,
better and lovelier clothes and clothes more suitable to adorn and
protect the darling bodies of men, better houses, and, above all,
better places for the worship of God and His proper praise; here,
alas! is commonly no more than a desire for release from the pains
thrust upon them by a selfish capitalism and, otherwise, no idea
more noble or even more human than to have *a good time*. For,
don't you see, in the Leisure State people won't really *love* the
"good things" they will enjoy in such plenty. They won't love
them in the sense that they will see them and use them as *holy*
things, things in which and by which God is manifest. In reality
they will despise everything. Things will be made only for pass-
ing enjoyment, to be scrapped when no longer enjoyable. Hence
the awful problem, even now, of the dumping ground for old
motor-cars; hence the problem of discarded razor blades. . . . It
is all a great illusion; the release from work does not and will
not mean the love of a good life and of good things; it does not
mean the City of God; it means, at the best, an impossible angelism and, at the worst, an impossible aestheticism, the worship
of the pleasure of sensation.

CHAPTER XXII

SECULAR AND SACRED IN
MODERN HISTORY

THE working man, the "hireling," the factory hand is still a very important person; there are still quite a large number of labourers, and the labourer's point of view is necessarily radically different from any other. No one to-day identifies the working man, the hireling, the labourer, with either artist or manufacturer. The factory hand is not expected to be an artist; he is not expected to share the responsibility or risks of the manufacturer, the man of business (and he seldom desires to do so), and it was only after much shedding of blood that he was allowed to have any part in politics. The banding together of labourers for the purpose of withstanding the vile tyranny of employers was for a long time illegal. The wretched hirelings were treated with every kind of cruelty and indecency, and their struggles for redress were met with shootings and hangings and transportation.

It is not necessary to describe the state of affairs in detail, because the divorce of art from industry is in its origin chiefly a matter of the degradation of the peasantry, the destruction of the small workshops, and the suppression of the craftsman (working personally for his personal customers) by the system of factory and machine production instituted solely for the sake of monetary gain.

And, in spite of everything, the idea that the artist represents the working man, the labourer, even the hireling, is not too fantastically absurd. Both are normally engaged in making things.

Both are normally workers with their hands. Both are normally paid for what they do and not paid if they don't do it. (In this respect unlike either the man of business or the politician.) Both are commonly instructed as to what is required of them before they begin working. The only difference between them is that the artist is responsible for the form and quality of what his deeds effect; he is the responsible workman, he had responsibility and would be insulted if he were denied it; but the workman, the labourer, the hireling, the factory hand, has been, as the theologian puts it, reduced to *a sub-human condition of intellectual irresponsibility;* he neither *has* responsibility nor does he now *desire* it. He is too deeply corrupted by his serfdom. The hireling flieth because he *is* a hireling. What was formerly his disgrace is now his privilege.

In spite of this great, this fundamental, difference between artist and labourer to-day, I shall claim to represent both. For, in spite of this difference, they are the same species of being. It is not the artist's fault if, after a century and a half of machine facture, he is reduced to the position of a mere designer. (I am thinking, of course, of the artist engaged in the production of the necessaries of life—food, clothing, shelter, furniture, and household utensils.) . . .

I say it is not the artist's fault if he is reduced to being a mere designer. And it is not the labourer's fault if he has been reduced to being merely instrumental, a tooth on a wheel, a sentient part of the machinery. Artists and workmen are the same species; some of them, specially gifted or specially favoured, have been set aside to design things which they never make; some of them, the greater number, the descendants of the dispossessed peasantry, who flocked to the towns in the time of the Enclosure Acts, or who came there as a consequence of the destruction of agriculture for the benefit, as Mr Chamberlain frankly admits, of export trade, these men and women, *not* specially gifted or specially favoured, are the rank and file of more or less emasculated factory hands. The designer draws what he never makes. The *hand* minds the machine which makes what he never designs.

Thus we have the divorce of art and industry. Some advocate a trial marriage between them as though art and industry were too young things only recently met, of whom it was difficult to judge whether they would be happy together. But it would be more accurate to liken them to a couple whom God has joined . . . and man has put asunder.

During the last hundred years there has been much discussion of the bearings of industrialism on the conditions of the labourer. The history of trade unionism supplies much cognate matter. The British Institute of Industrial Art said in one of its earliest manifestoes that never in the whole course of our rough island history (or words to that effect) had it been more necessary than it is now to swell the volume of foreign trade, and that, to this end, artists and manufacturers ought to collaborate. The idea that *art* is something which, like sugar on a pill, makes industrial products go down better—and, in spite of everything that the critics may say, that is, and must be the primary point of view of the man of business—it must be so because, as Sir Percy Bates so rightly and frankly states, the production of dividends is the first duty of those who control industrial enterprises, they owe it as a first duty to their investors—so the idea that *art* is something which enables the manufacturer to put his goods across has been much discussed.

There has also been much discussion of the matter from the point of view of the consumer. Faced with the manifest discontent of the labourers and with their no less manifest degradation —faced with the manifest inferiority of the best industrial products compared with the best products of hand craftsmanship—in those lines of production where comparison could be made—for example: articles of food, clothing, furniture, building, kitchen gadgets, pots and pans—faced with these things it has been obviously necessary, especially as dividends depended on it, to make as much as possible of the advantages, supposed or real, accruing to the consumer from the great multiplication of goods and services which industrialism has made possible. If you can't boost quality at least you can boost quantity; and from a quantitative

point of view industrialism leaves extraordinarily little to be desired. How often has it been pointed out that the labourer of
to-day has more, much more, tinned food than his ancestors ever
had home-made bread? . . .

Then, again, from the quantitative point of view: many things
are now obtainable which would otherwise be unknown. You
could make a typewriter or a fountain pen by hand, but only ex-
cessively rich people could afford to possess such things. To make
such things available to *you and me* there simply must be industrialism. Wireless, the cinema, motor-cars, clocks and watches,
electric light, bathrooms—all these things which even very rich
and important people could not formerly possess, not even kings
or cardinals, are now the ordinary possessions of clerks and
scullery-maids. All this aspect of industrialism has been given
publicity. What without advertisement and one thing and another we are now in the position of drug addicts—we couldn't
give up these luxuries if we tried. Luxuries have become necessities. . . .

Then, again, there are the *culture* people. These are very different from the *arts and crafts*. They think industrialism is "quite
all right," their only complaint is that the increase of leisure,
sometimes realistically called *unemployment,* which mechanization of industry produces and is designed to produce (for there's
no point in using machinery if you're not going to reduce your
costs, and labour is the biggest cost as well as the most difficult
to deal with)—the increase of leisure does not spell an increase of
culture. This is very distressing to many well-meaning people, and
the matter is receiving much attention. And all these various ap-
proaches to the matter are extremely interesting and useful.

But there is one aspect of the matter, and that, surprising
though it may seem, the most important aspect, which has not
been discussed at all—that is the relation of art and industry to
holiness.

I say this might seem surprising; but, of course, the reason is
obvious. The divorce of art from industry is a fact, but it is not

166

an independent fact. The divorce of art from industry is the consequence of the divorce of business from morals, from ethics, from metaphysics, from any kind of wisdom, from goodness, from beauty; in fact, the whole affair of human life has been secularized.

The history of this change, for change it is, and historically a most abnormal occurrence, is no affair of ours on this occasion. You can see for yourselves that it is a fact—and countless common phrases affirm it. When did we first use the phrases, "charity school" and "cold as charity"? When did the words, "a home child," first come to mean a child without a home, or brought up in an institution? When was it first said that religion is your private affair and nothing to do with your business? When did portraits of our mistresses displace images of saints in our sitting-rooms? When were the funds of working men's guilds commandeered by the State because they were used to support religious observances? When did the facts that we can arrive by weighing and measuring come to seem more important and trustworthy than the truths of reason and revelation?

The answers to such questions do not matter now. I simply repeat the fact that human life is now more or less completely secularized. In such circumstances it is not surprising that art and industry are divorced from holiness and that that aspect of the matter has received little or no discussion.

None the less, that is the business we must now apply ourselves to, for it is self-evident that if there *be* such a thing as holiness, if the idea of holiness is not absurd, if holiness exists, then it is and must be the most important thing of all. Ultimately nothing else matters. For holiness is man's last end. It cannot be otherwise. If there *be* holiness then it must be that to which all things converge. The opposite cannot be true. Nevertheless, when we consider the basis, the origins of our industrialism, it is not surprising that the notion of holiness should be pushed into the background. For, if we do not deny its existence, we are quite indifferent to it. We do not desire *un*holiness. We are simply too busy, too wrapped up in business to bother about it.

It is quite understandable, in this world of business, in which, as stated by its own leaders, the first object is the production of dividends, that the relations between industry and holiness should not be in the forefront. The *world* is not concerned with man's last end, or with any other final thing. It is only concerned with a more or less hand to mouth adjustment of business rivalries, quarrels in a sort of thieves' kitchen. . . .

Now, in order to understand the relation of sacred and secular in modern industry, it is necessary to understand the nature of art itself, of industry, of human labour, of humanity, of man. I affirm, then, the general nature of *art* is personal, and sacred, whereas the general nature of *industry* is impersonal and secular. These things follow from the proper meaning of these words— proper, that is, according to their ancient meaning and their still common use in the conversation of common people. Art is skill, the skill of man, the skill of man in doing and making. And a work of *art*, an artifact, is something made by a man. And as men don't, any more than other animals do, make things for no reason at all, for no purpose at all, it has come to be said: "a work of art is that which fits"—fits the purpose for which it is made. And thus again it is said: "art is the well-making of what needs making." But there is bad art as well as good. Some things are less well made than others. Some needs are less worthy than others, nevertheless, we should hesitate to call that thing a work of art which serves no purpose at all, or having a purpose does not in the least serve it.

And so we have the art of a cook and of a dentist, of a smith and of a carpenter, and all such common arts. And so we have the less common arts, so called *fine* arts, of the painter and of the poet, of the sculptor, the musician, and the architect. The common arts have been almost entirely done away with in our society of machine facture; it has come about that the word "art" is now almost exclusively associated, at least in fashionable literary circles, with the *fine* arts. And thus, painters and poets and such, having no ordinary job of work to do, being, like those labourers in the Gospel, idle, because no man has hired them—such people use the word "art" to mean, not human skill in making things, but the ability of certain special people, specially trained or specially gifted, to exhibit in paint or stone or word or sound, their special sensibilities and fine feelings—aesthetics, that is, beauty-mongering. In spite of all this the word "art" still means what it originally meant, it still means the work of man as such.

And being work of man, it partakes of man's nature; this is self-evident; but what is the nature of man? . . .

I shall assume the existence of God. And I assume a general belief in God's existence. Therefrom, I may affirm that man is God's creature. Man, child of God, and, if child, *heir also*. Child of God, made in God's image, therefore having free will and therefore having responsibility for his acts and the intended consequences of his acts, having a rational nature and being, therefore, a person, and if child, *heir also*. Therefore called, having a vocation. And so it necessarily follows that all that he does and all that he makes must be done and made in the light of that vocation. And in a general way it is true to say that that vocation, that calling, is to *him,* to him *personally,* to collaborate with God in creating, to make all things good, that is to say, beautiful, that is to say, holy. For the good is holiness desired. The beautiful is holiness visible, holiness seen, heard, touched, holiness tasted—"O taste and see how gracious the Lord is"—holiness, *smell* of Paradise.

Such is the common vocation of man. All men are called. All men are sacred persons. All their works are holy. That is to say all the works are holy which are done by men in the exercise of their human personality. For that personality is of its very nature holy. So it is that we say: "the general nature of art is personal and sacred."

And the general nature of industry is impersonal and secular. Industry is not of its nature specifically either human or holy. It does not partake of the nature of man as such. "Man is born to labour; the bird to fly," but it is as the bird flies that man labours;

it is in accordance with the condition of his material existence. . . .

The word "industry" is rightly applied to the labour of the bee and the ant, the bird building its nest, as much as to that of men in factories and mines. Industry means labour as such, the simple exercise of strength. It requires persistence but not necessarily love, or initiative or imagination or creativeness—and therefore nothing specially human or personal. Thus we use the word to-day when we speak of the chief enterprises of industrial production.

In these enterprises men are not employed as men, but as instruments, tools, sentient parts of machines. Their labour is a means to the end which the owners and directors of the enterprises have in view—and that end is economic, the production of wealth. And, from the point of view of the economist, the criterion of wealth is utility—and the criterion of utility is saleability.

So industrial labour has for its end not the fulfilment of the personal vocation of the labourer, but the production of profit for those who employ him, who sell the goods that his labour has been instrumental in producing.

And as industrial labour is not directed to the personal ends of the labourer, it is of its nature secular and not sacred. There is nothing either venerable or holy in its products. Thus it naturally comes about that we do not venerate them. We have no compunction in destroying them; we have no desire to make them last or to hand them on as heirlooms to our children. Thus, though we are certainly in no danger of idolatry, we are equally deprived of both joy in labour and of opportunity or occasion to praise God in it.

And as regards the labour itself—there is nothing venerable about that either. "The dignity of labour" is a phrase having no meaning in an industrial society. Or, if any meaning still attaches to it, it is but the dregs of the meaning it had in what you might call Old Testament times. The labour of a shepherd in the lambing season, the labour of the ploughman, of the mason, of the maker of sacred images—all such labours are venerable, and venerable because of a dependence upon the personal will and reason of the labourer. So also is the labour of the housewife. Such labours are responsible for the form and quality of what their deeds effect. Such labourers are persons. And as persons they serve their fellow men. But in a machine shop, *on the belt,* or as one of a sort of chain-gang performing repetitive operations, there is no such dependence upon the will and reason of the worker, and so we very rightly replace men by machines whenever that is possible. And if machines can be made to mind machines, we shall be still more pleased.

There is no doubt that that is the sort of world we now live in, and it would be quite impossible either to do away with industrialism or even to alter it radically, either immediately or quickly, even if a ruling class of persons would wish to do so. The dislocation and distress would be disastrous. . . .

Suppose any factory owner were to take literally the teachings of the papal encyclicals and act on the doctrine that a living wage to the labourer—meaning by that not merely a starvation or subsistence wage, the lowest a man can be compelled to accept, but a wage sufficient to enable him to own a house of his own and bring up a normal family and save a bit for old age—I say if we were to act on the doctrine that a living wage to the labourer was the first charge on industry and should be paid before any overhead charges be paid to the subscribers of capital—the result, it is well known, would be disaster. Not only would capital not be forthcoming, but the business would be made bankrupt. Industrial enterprise cannot pay such wages.

These things being understood, there is no suggestion in anything I am saying that I think it possible to put back the clock or that we can become Ancient Britons. . . . It is, in fact, no more possible to go back than it would be to go forward in the direction of an even greater and more complete mechanization of industry.

My position is merely that of one who happens to see what that direction is and what is its end. . . .

No, there is no putting back of clocks. The clock of our civilization will run on, just as the clock of Rome ran on—and ran down. Can you not imagine the complacent councillor in the ancient Forum about the year A.D. 15 saying to some upstart person like myself: "You can't put the clock back, my boy." But had I been there then, with the knowledge we have now, I might have said: "No, no indeed, sir, but you may be interested to know that in exactly three hundred years from now, year 315, Rome will be sacked, and for fifteen days on end there will be nothing in your noble streets but fire and murder and rape and plundering. That's what you're heading for, noble and complacent councillor, that's what the grandeur of Rome will come to." So, we may confidently anticipate, that will be the end of our pride and dominion —our conquest of nature, our application of science to industry.

The decay and eventual disappearance of industrialism is inevitable. The motive which sustains it is not man's vocation to holiness, and holiness is necessarily the ultimate value in human affairs.

That holiness is the ultimate value, if we admit the existence of holiness, is obvious. It is obvious also that our industrialism had no such origin as the promotion of holiness. It is equally obvious that no such motive inspires it now. . . . Nor have either masters or men the idea that the most important product of their factories is the men and women who work in them—that all things are made to minister to *persons,* and therefore partake of the nature and the end of personality. "In our great factories," said Ruskin—that great man whom we scorn because his economics were founded on the Gospels and not on Adam Smith, because he preferred Bethlehem to Lanarkshire, "In our factories we fabricate everything except men." We may now go farther; we may say that in our factories we make all things for sale and destroy the men and women who are to buy them. To speak of the divorce of art from industry is, after all, only a way of speaking of the disintegration. And disintegration is only a long word for death. . . .

Work is the means to living. The two things are inseparable. Recreation is a means to working and not the object for which we work. The object of recreation is to enable us to return to work refreshed, renewed, revived. . . .

But in order to take such a view of work, the work must be good, it must be worth doing. Moreover, it must exercise our personality, it must be the work of persons. This is the fundamental evil of industrialism.

It has depersonalized work. It has disintegrated the worker. It has made the work the least interesting, because the least personal part of his life. It has created a state of things in which nothing is expected from work, but the pay for doing it, and all the happiness of living is relegated to the time when we are not working.

Although the inhumanity and unholiness of our society, of our industrialism, must inevitably bring its appropriate disaster—war, pestilence, and famine, battle, murder, and sudden death—and in the not very distant future (*perhaps I should point out that I am not in the least referring to the recent or present crisis in European politics. I am speaking of the general tendency, not of particular movements*)—nevertheless, I do not stand here as a·fatalistic prophet. Though the policy of "eat, drink, and be merry, for to-morrow we die," becomes increasingly more attractive and wins more and more adherents, there are still some who can see the wood as well as the trees, and can suggest, if not a way out, at least some principles which will be useful and· necessary in the new dark age which is upon us. . . .

And it seems to me that, at the risk of giving offence, I must put before you a principle which is of primary and permanent importance—both in the government of states and in such a matter as the relations of art and industry.

That principle is the principle of POVERTY.

But first of all, I must make it clear that I am not speaking of destitution, want. . . . Nor am I referring to the poverty of the poor clerk or small shopkeeper who must needs keep up a respectable appearance, and yet live in a state of perpetual insecurity and harassment. These are not the poverty I refer to when I speak of the *principle* of poverty. I am not talking about *unholy* but *holy* poverty. It is not poverty as an evil that I mean.

For when we speak of *chastity* we do not mean something evil —we do not mean the evil chastity of those who would but cannot marry. When we speak of *obedience* we do not mean something evil. We do not mean slavery. We do not mean the evil obedience of the workman who desires human responsibility and is denied it. And so it is not *evil* poverty I am speaking about—the evil poverty endured by men and women who are denied their just human needs.

I am talking about poverty as a *good*—just as chastity is a good and obedience is a good. I am talking of that poverty which as the theologians say, is "the rational attitude in a material world, that virtue which regulates our attitude to material things." I am talking of *holy* poverty, which is that same virtue strengthened and inspired by love. That poverty which is a necessary good, the poverty of the spirit which is the crown and seal of the Kingdom of Heaven, that spiritual poverty which, like all spiritual things, bears its fruit in human life and works, and must bear fruit or perish.

But it is only in love that this poverty can be embraced—like that chastity—like that obedience.

I am assuming that you will bear with me if I thus seem to preach you a sermon. I am trying to probe to the roots of the matter. Art and Industry! There is something wrong in our society —there is, in my opinion, something *radically* wrong. How can such corruption fail to affect our art and industry? How can a discussion of art and industry fail to concern itself with the radical evils of our time? It is not window-dressing we are concerned with, but the very basis of human industry and production.

And it must be pointed out that though I presume to speak as a christian, what I am saying is true even of non-christian and pre-christian periods and peoples. In all times and places where the common arts of men have flourished, that is to say, flowered and fruited, the exuberance of a merely animal nature has at all times and places needed to be curbed and repressed, and *especially* the insubordination of men of business. When that repression has been successful—as in medieval India no less than in medieval Europe—in the South Sea Islands and Peru—in Persia or Assyria or Egypt—then the common arts have flourished. . . .

But I say the best and most perfect way is the way of love. For though we are rational beings, yet we use our reason so rarely and fitfully and with so rash a carelessness, without training or discipline; we follow our prejudices and predilections with such confidence and impudence, that any appeal based on reason is unlikely to be successful. Moreover, the lovely has a wider reference than the reasonable. . . .

In a general way the world, for all its ungodliness, believes in God. He is called Father—to designate the fact that we know Him as a person. And this is true of all religions.

And, obviously, to know the will of our Father is the first duty of intelligent children. There is nothing arbitrary about this—it is plain common sense. It would be stupid to do anything else. And if this is the basis of domestic life, it is just as obviously the basis of social life and therefore of human politics. Therefore it is that we say, echoing William Blake: *"Religion is politics and politics is brotherhood."* For without religion—that is, a knowledge of God's will and an answer to the countryman's question: "What's it all blooming well for?" there can be no real politics, but only the shifting sands of irrational selfishness and violence. Perpetual warfare and the resulting disorder and misery cannot be God's will for men. It cannot be in accord with our nature—child of God, heir also—to desire disorder, pain, disease, ugliness, and insecurity.

Religion is politics and politics is brotherhood. For the only possible first principle of political action must be the brotherhood of men. Attempt to maintain the opposite—it is absurd. Who could seriously affirm that the object of human politics was to enable thieves and robbers and usurers to carry on undisturbed? That may seem to be the chief business of national governments to-day. But who would admit it?

Child of God, therefore children of God, therefore brothers. All wars are civil wars. The doctrine of sovereign states is superstition.

Politics is brotherhood—how to contrive the hierarchy of men. How to arrange our affairs so that the better shall not be at the mercy of the worse. How to ensure that the merely cunning and grasping shall not reduce their brothers to slavery. How to reduce the man of money and controller of credit to their proper subordination.

And brotherhood is poverty—that is the secret. Revealed in religions and, in spite of countless saints and prophets, hardly yet known to men.

We think that things can be put right by fire and slaughter or by Act of Parliament, or by revolution. Because people have failed to win the strong to reason, people proclaim with Mussolini that "freedom is a concession of the state." Because wicked men have sequestered to their private aggrandisement the riches that are designed for the common good, therefore people say with Karl Marx and his followers, "all individual appropriation of the means of production is evil." We forget that the hireling flieth because he is a hireling, and not because he is evil—and that individual appropriation of the means of production is ordained for the good of the work to be done and not for the glorification of private owners.

For we work not only for our own good, but for that of our brothers. And that they may be better served, it is necessary that we serve them personally. And how can we thus serve if we are without responsibility for the quality of what we do or make? And how can we have responsibility if we have no control? And how can we control what does not belong to us, but is the impersonal and irresponsible possession of an anonymous collection of joint-stock investors?

Brotherhood is poverty—imagine the opposite! Let us say that, in order to achieve brotherhood, we will bend all our energies to the job of getting rich quickly. We will worship those who have much and we will despise the poor. We will so order our parliaments that rich men control law making—that poor men shall have nothing but votes. That the City of London and the Bank of England shall control British farming in the interests of foreign investment. We will so arrange the business of production that those who control capital shall be able to reduce those who labour to a sub-human condition of intellectual irresponsibility, thus causing them perpetual shame and inexpressible discontent, so sowing the seeds of violence and hatred. And having done all these things, we will attempt appeasement by means of a larger police force—officered by the sons of the rich—and greater and greater armaments so that "during their periodical strikes they may be shot down by their own sons the moment they lose patience" (P. Kropotkin). Such politics may enable a few to acquire riches—they will certainly not achieve human brotherhood.

As I have said, these things are true of all nations and civilizations. They are explicit in the teaching of Christianity, if not in the practice of Christians. And if there is one thing more certain than anything else in this teaching, it is the *teaching of poverty*. *To go without, to give up, to lose rather than gain, to have little rather than much*—that is its positive teaching. Blessed are the poor in spirit. The humble, the common man, the common workman, simple women, mothers of children. "How hard it is for a rich man to enter Heaven." But in spite of all this—in spite of the obvious failure of rich men's politics—we refuse to base our life and work on such teaching.

We think it is only a counsel of perfection—that it doesn't apply to us—to ordinary men and women. We still fail to see that it is plain human wisdom as well as divine revelation.

All our politics are founded on a denial of this gospel. Our capitalist society is based solely upon the notion that those who have riches have the right and privilege to get richer still; that those who have nothing must be enslaved or exploited or—"employed," and until such times as machines have made their existence unnecessary; that the desire of gain is the only possible motive for production. How is it conceivable in such a world that things made shall be holy?

This, then, is my conclusion:

Whatever be the immediate necessity—however inevitable be the doom which is upon us—the ultimate aim of politics must be the encouragement and protection of human personality. Politics, whether of production or distribution or consumption, which, whatever their success in promoting quantity, nevertheless destroy or tend to destroy the full responsibility of individual men and women, stand condemned. The production of good things depends upon the personal control of the actual living workmen who make them. Not otherwise can men be well served or God praised.

Hence it is inevitable that this industrialism will eventually decay and disappear; for it is inconceivable that a method of production so sub-human will for much longer content us, or that a control so impersonal as that of finance can much longer be endured.

Meanwhile those who are convinced of these things, in spite of their small numbers and their powerlessness, can but say so and, in their personal lives and as members of society, promote the resurgence of personal control by the workers and the discouragement of the veneration now given to the rich and to riches, and the "debunking" of the quantitative glories of industrialism. For both logically and intuitively it is obvious that the sacred should govern the secular, and that our present society, in which the secular governs the sacred, is both inhuman and unholy. "He that loses his life shall save it." This is, indeed, the Christianity we still profess. This is revelation—it is also common sense. And it is the only basis for any marriage of art and industry.

CHAPTER XXIII

AND WHO WANTS PEACE?

(An address made at Kingsway Hall, London, 11 Nov. 1936)

I AM asked to speak as a Catholic, a Roman Catholic, and as an artist.

Certainly I will speak as a Catholic, as a Christian.

But I will not speak as an "artist," because I don't believe in the distinction.

An artist is supposed to be a person who makes things for the sake of beauty, as though beautiful things were something special.

But in our society we assume that most men make things simply according to the dictates of greed—they call it "business" or "economics" or, when they are speaking at their annual dinners, they call it "the service of their fellow-men."

And in our society we assume that only a few special men, men with special gifts and men specially trained, make things for any other reason.

The chief thing we assume these special men to work for is beauty.

For, strange as it may seem, the worship of beauty is the very heart and centre of the business man's religion.

That is why we have picture galleries and art schools and the Royal Academy and Royal Society of Sculptors, and the National Gallery.

That is why we make painters of pictures and poets and other such people lords and knights—because we worship beauty and give it special honour—honour undreamed of in medieval England, although there was no dearth of painters and poets in the middle ages, a fact which is well known because we cherish their works—give them special honour—in our museums and picture galleries and libraries.

. . . . . .

But I will not speak as an "artist," because I repudiate the title.

I do not live in a Christian world, but I will try to speak as a Christian.

Now this modern worship of beauty has an intimate connection with the object of this meeting—the promotion of peace in our time.

What is the connection?

It is clear. It is this:

We worship beauty because we have isolated beauty.

We have cut beauty off from everyday life, and from everyday work and everyday things. We have made it something special, rare, expensive.

And what is left? What kind of world is it in which ordinary people work and live?

It is the world of business—that fearsome world in which every man is his neighbour's enemy—in which it is an absolute rule of success that every man must try to circumvent his brother.

It is a world of which the very essence is war.

They say charity begins at home. So does war.

There is no possible chance of obtaining a world in which charity rules between nations unless we have already obtained a world in which charity rules between man and man.

There is no possible chance of obtaining a world in which peace rules between nations unless we have already obtained a world in which peace rules between men of business.

. . . . . .

There are those who would persuade us that the causes of war in our time are racial jealousies and the need of national expansion.

They would have us think that the French and the Germans and the Russians are primitive races like the Picts and Scots—hordes of hungry ruffians moved by greed and jealousy.

Doubtless there are such greeds and jealousies—there have been from the beginning and will be to the end.

But to-day these things are not the causes of war; they are emotions which men of business exploit. If you wish men to fight and destroy one another you must arouse their hatreds and jealousies—you must fan them to flame by propaganda.

To-day the causes of war are almost entirely business causes—that is to say, money causes.

The whole world is scrambling and grabbing for money—for markets and oil-fields, and coal-fields, and "spheres of influence," and "concessions."

But the spirit of money-making begins at home—in England as much as in Germany or France or Italy or Russia.

And it begins in small businesses as much as in big ones.

For the little shopkeeper wants to be a big shopkeeper and the little business envies big business.

.   .   .   .   .   .

However much it may appear that racial hatreds are the cause of war, they are not the real cause.

For we must remember that modern wars are not fought with sticks and stones—but with the most stupendously costly apparatus the world has ever known.

The Japanese hate the Russians, we are told.

The Americans hate the Japanese.

The French hate the Germans.

The Germans, to complete the circle, hate the Russians.

Personally, I don't believe half these things.

But whatever else is true, it is true that none of these nations can fight one another to-day without the most enormous expense for guns and aeroplanes and poisons.

How can these things be paid for unless bankers and financiers put up the money?

181

And in a world ruled by money it is self-evident that such expenses
would not be incurred unless someone was finding it profitable.

．　　　．　　　．　　　．　　　．

Consider our own war finances.

What is the National Debt but war finance?

And what is that debt but an immense tribute to money-lenders?

Every penny paid in income-tax is usury on war loan.

A million Englishmen gave their lives in the last war.

What did the financiers give?

They gave nothing. They only lent their money at interest.

A million Englishmen gave their lives.

What did the traders give?

They gave nothing—they sold stores and munitions at immense
profit to themselves.

They tell us to-day about a return to prosperity!

What is that prosperity due to?

They say it is due to increased employment.

What is that employment due to but to a vast increase in
armaments?

These armaments will be paid for by taxation—either directly
by taxation or by taxation to pay the interest on new war
loans.

And these taxes will be paid by us and by our children and our
children's children.

．　　　．　　　．　　　．　　　．

Is it not obvious that racial hatreds cannot be the cause of modern
wars?

For however much the races hated one another they could not
fight with modern weapons unless financiers put up the money
to pay for them.

And however much politicians begged for money the financiers
would not lend unless they could see the interest on their
money.

And how can they see the interest on their money unless there is increased trading—that is to say, more money-making—more coal, more oil, more "spheres of influence," more "concessions"?

More exploitation of native labour on cotton and rubber plantations.

More exploitation of British emigrants in the mechanized wheat-lands of Australia and Canada.

· · · · · ·

I am to speak as a Christian and as an artist.

I refuse to speak as an artist—because I am ashamed to be called one.

And I am almost ashamed to speak as a Christian.

And I am almost more ashamed to speak as a Roman Catholic.

For it seems to me true to say that we Christians are more to blame than anyone else in the world—both individually and collectively—for the present state of affairs:

Peace is the tranquillity of order. Is it not the special mission of Christians to promote peace and the charity between men upon which alone peace can be built?

And yet it might be said that Christians and, in a special way, Christian ministers (of all denominations) have been the foremost recruiting sergeants.

They have been the first to be deceived by the plausible propaganda of politicians and the masters of politicians, the men of business and financiers.

Who has not heard the sermons of army chaplains?

Who does not remember the part played by bishops and parish clergy?

Who does not remember the ways of vicars' wives during the war of 1914-1918?

And since that war!—Has it yet become notorious that Christian ministers are in the front rank of those who work for peace?

· · · · · ·

183

But it is not only the Christian ministers who appear to promote and praise war—though they are more conspicuous by reason of their public position.

The laity, the Christian laity, and especially the Christian press, the newspapers, are notorious war-mongers.

Like the young man in the gospel, they turn away sorrowful from all talk of peace—because they have great possessions.

They are men of business first and Christians after.

They are imperialists, they believe in empire, and foreign possessions, and foreign trade, and investments, in exactly the same way as their non-Christian fellows.

We accuse the Russians of denying God. . . .

But who have been more conspicuously ungodly than the Christians? And who have been more bloodthirsty?

How can this monstrous situation be explained?

I think there is only one charitable explanation.

It is due to ignorance, an ignorance fostered by our traditions— traditions which keep us entirely out of touch with the realities of the modern world.

We still fondly believe that wars are patriotic affairs made in defence of king and country, the homes of the people, and the religion of our fathers.

We are still blandly ignorant of the real nature of the developments of modern industrialism.

We are everywhere dependent, or imagine ourselves to be, upon the goodwill and the bounty of the rich and powerful—and we scarcely dare call in question the methods of modern money-making. We dare not open our eyes to the tyranny of finance—a tyranny which, in the words of Pope Leo XIII, places upon "the broken down and suffering multitudes a yoke little better than slavery itself," so that, in the words of the present pope, "those who control credit (i.e., the financiers), control the very life-blood of the people and no one dares breathe against their goodwill."

. . . . . .

We do not see this thing called war in proper perspective.

We still see it decked out with romantic trappings of the small quarrels of the past.

We are still doped by the superstition that wars are fought for honour and glory.

We are blind to the fact that, in a world ruled by financiers, the only object of war is financial advantage.

And we are blind to the fact that those who reap the advantage never do the fighting.

We do not see that it is more courageous to die as a "pacifist" than to win as a poisoner.

We do not see that you cannot gather figs off thistles.

We do not see that you cannot have just wars in a world in which justice does not rule at home.

.   .   .   .   .   .

But, in spite of my shame, I speak as a Christian.

For, whatever the ignorance or apathy or negligence of our pastors, whatever our own ignorance and negligence, however vile the press—the law of Christ is the law of peace.

And I say this:

War as we know it to-day, war as it has come to be, is no longer such as Christian men can take part in.

We will no longer be misled by false propaganda.

We will no longer be the dupes of those who, under the guise of defending the fatherland, seek only commercial aggrandizement.

And I say this:

War as we know it to-day is not only such as no Christian can take part in, it is also such as no mere man, no mere human being, can take part in.

It has become bestial, it has become inhuman, it has become the wildest folly and imbecility.

It has, in fact, taken on the full character of our industrialism.

Like our industrialism, like our world of factories and big business and money-making, war is now a thing outside all the laws of God—outside all equity, all decency.

Like our industrialism, it is impervious to shame, monstrous in its vulgarity, a surrender to all the lusts of devils.

Are our fellow-men rats and fleas that we should attempt to exterminate them with poison?

I cannot tell whether to rage at the enormity of the sin or to weep at such a foul surrender of human reason.

In any case it is clear—whatever the consequences, we refuse to take part in it. . . . We refuse.

. . . . . .

It used to be said in public schools that there are "things no fellow should do."

And if you refer to the book of Deuteronomy, chapter 25, verses 11 and 12, you will find the eternal warrant for such refusal:

"If two men have words together, and one begin to fight against the other, and the other's wife, willing to deliver her husband out of the hand of the stronger, shall put forth her hand and take him by the secrets, thou shalt cut off her hand, neither shalt thou be moved with any pity in her regard." (Douay Version.)

. . . . . .

I am not saying no war was ever justified.

I am not saying that the use of force is always wrong.

I am saying that war to-day has become bestial and therefore impossible.

Why should men give themselves over to bestiality in the name of patriotism and at the bidding of financiers and poisoners?

Are there no things a man may refuse to do?

Modern war having come to be what it is, all talk about patriotism and the defence of civilization is irrelevant.

"There are some things no fellow should do."

. . . . . .

What is the alternative of which we are so afraid? Do we fear the
destruction of our cities?
>But are the pomp and squalor of London and Manchester and
>Glasgow and Cardiff anything to be proud of?
Do we fear the killing of our wives and children?
>But they would not be killed if we did not resist.
Are we afraid of national humiliation, are we afraid to be hum-
bled?
>But it is written, "Blessed are the meek for they shall inherit
>the earth . . .!"
Are we afraid of poverty?
>But it is precisely poverty which as Christians we should wel-
>come.
>>There will be no peace, there can be no peace, there cannot
>>possibly be any peace, while wealth, comfort, riches are
>>the ideal we set before ourselves.

.   .   .   .   .   .

>"I was playing golf one day
>When the Germans landed
>All our soldiers ran away
>All our ships were stranded.
>Thinking then of *England's shame*
>Very nearly spoilt my game."

What is this thing called "England's shame"?
>That we have surrendered our agriculture in order to sell ma-
>chinery and machine-made things all over the world.
>That our country is devastated by vast and squalid cities.
>That we think the only object of working is to have money
>and leisure to enjoy ourselves.
>That we are the biggest money-lenders in the world and draw
>usury from the ends of the earth.
These are the things to be ashamed of.
Or are we afraid of losing our foreign possessions?
>But it is not we who are afraid of such losses.

It is our rulers—our financiers and traders.

It is they who promote wars and profit by them.

. . . . .

In business jargon there is a thing called "the law of diminishing returns."

Is it not now abundantly clear that modern mechanized warfare has long passed the limits which could conceivably make wars either profitable, or endurable, or forgivable?

Modern war is a remedy worse than any conceivable disease.

During the last war they called conscientious objectors cowards.

It was the grossest lie.

But now cowardice becomes a high virtue.

Is it virtue to be afraid of nothing?

On the contrary: it is virtue to be afraid of the just anger of God.

It is virtue to be afraid to continue any longer such bestiality, such ignominy, such imbecility, such childishness.

And I say:

War, war between civilized nations, is finished.

It is finished

—because we have finished with it.

BOOKS WRITTEN BY ERIC GILL [1]

1918 SCULPTURE. An Essay reprinted from *The Highway*, June, 1917, Douglas Pepler, Ditchling, Sussex. 21 pp.

1921 SONGS WITHOUT CLOTHES. Being a dissertation on the Song of Solomon; with a preface by Vincent McNabb. St. Dominic's Press, Ditchling, Sussex. (Same; Chaucer Head, N. Y.)

1923 SCULPTURE. An Essay on Stone-cutting. St. Dominic's Press, Ditchling, Sussex. With illustration and device. (Same; Chaucer Head, N. Y.)

WAR MEMORIAL. (Welfare Handbook No. 10). St. Dominic's Press, Ditchling, Sussex. 12 pp. 2 engravings.

1926 ID QUOD VISUM PLACET. A practical test of the beautiful. The Golden Cockerel Press, Waltham Saint Lawrence, Berkshire. 19 pp. 2 engravings.

1927 ARCHITECTURE AND SCULPTURE. A lecture. Faulkner, Manchester.

ART AND LOVE. Douglas Cleverdon, Bristol, 26 pp. with 6 engravings. (260 copies.)

CHRISTIANITY AND ART. Francis Walterson, Capel-y-ffin, Abergavenny.

CONTEMPORARY BRITISH ARTISTS. Benn, London.

1928 ART AND PRUDENCE. An Essay. The Golden Cockerel Press, Waltham Saint Lawrence, Berkshire. (Also published by Random House, N. Y., 1928.) 18 pp. with 2 illustrations.

FUTURE OF SCULPTURE. (Privately printed for the author by the Lanston Monotype Corporation.) With map.

1929 ART AND NONSENSE AND OTHER ESSAYS. (Twenty-four essays.) Cassell & Co. & Francis Walterson, London. 324 pp. 1 engraving. (Reprinted in a cheap edition in 1934 as No. 17 of 'Cassell's Pocket Library' with a different engraving.)

ART AND MANUFACTURE. (Handworkers' Pamphlets No. 4.) New Handworkers' Gallery, London. 2 illustrations.

1 NOTE: This list is probably not complete. The publishers would be pleased to receive additions or corrections.

ENGRAVINGS BY ERIC GILL. A Selection of Engravings on Wood and Metal, representative of his work to the end of the year 1927 with a complete Chronological List of Engravings and a Preface by the Artist. 148 engravings. Douglas Cleverdon, Bristol. (A limited edition in three formats.)

1931 CLOTHES. An Essay upon the Nature and Significance of the Natural and Artificial Integuments Worn by Men and Women. Jonathan Cape, London. 196 pp. with 10 diagrams engraved by the Author.

CLOTHING WITHOUT CLOTH. An Essay on the Nude. The Golden Cockerel Press, Waltham Saint Lawrence, Berkshire. 18 pp. 4 woodcuts.

PRINTING AND PIETY. An Essay on life and works in the England of 1931, and particularly typography. Sheed & Ward, London. Illustrated. (Reprinted with an added chapter as *Typography* in a cheap edition in 1936 [136 pp.] and reissued in 1941 by J. M. Dent & Sons, Ltd. London.)

1932 SCULPTURE AND THE LIVING MODEL. With a wood engraving by the Author. Sheed & Ward, London. 24 pp.

1933 BEAUTY LOOKS AFTER HERSELF. (Thirteen essays.) Sheed & Ward, London. 253 pp.

UNEMPLOYMENT. (An Essay.) With a wood engraving by the author. Faber & Faber, Ltd., London, 32 pp.

1934 MONEY AND MORALS. (Three essays.) Faber & Faber, Ltd., London. With nine illustrations by Denis Tegetmeier. (Reprinted with an additional essay in 1937.)

THE LORD'S SONG. A Sermon. The Golden Cockerel Press, Waltham Saint Lawrence, Berkshire. 15 pp. 1 illustration.

ART AND A CHANGING CIVILIZATION. With appended articles by R. Heppenstall and G. M. Turnell. (No. 8 of 'The Twentieth-Century Library'.) John Lane, The Bodley Head Ltd., London, 158 pp.

ENGRAVINGS 1928-1933. By Eric Gill. Faber & Faber, Ltd., London. (Hague and Gill publication.) Preface by the engraver.

THREE BOOK TYPES. A Specimen of three book types designed by Eric Gill. (Printed for private circulation by Hague & Gill, High Wycombe, Bucks.)

1935 WORK AND LEISURE. (Three essays). Faber & Faber, Ltd., London. 142 pp.

1936 THE NECESSITY OF BELIEF. An enquiry into the nature of human certainty, the causes of scepticism and the grounds of morality, and a justification of the doctrine that the end is the beginning. Faber & Faber, Ltd., London. 354 pp.

1937 WORK AND PROPERTY. (Eight essays.) J. M. Dent & Sons, Ltd., London. 141 pp. Illustrated by Denis Tegetmeier.

TROUSERS AND THE MOST PRECIOUS ORNAMENT. Faber & Faber, Ltd., London. 22 pp.

SCULPTURE ON MACHINE-MADE BUILDINGS. (A Lecture.) City of Birmingham School of Printing. Birmingham.

1938 AND WHO WANTS PEACE? (Pax Pamphlets, No. 1.) James Clarke & Co., Ltd., London.

TWENTY-FIVE NUDES. Engravings; with an introduction. J. M. Dent & Sons, Ltd., London. 6 pp. 27 plates. (Hague and Gill publication.)

WORK AND CULTURE. A lecture given before the Royal Society of Arts, London, April, 1938. John Stephens, Newport, Rhode Island. 25 pp.

UNHOLY TRINITY. Pictures by Denis Tegetmeier. J. M. Dent & Sons, Ltd., London. 24 pp. (Hague and Gill publication.)

1939 SOCIAL JUSTICE AND THE STATIONS OF THE CROSS. Illustrated by the author. James Clarke & Co., Ltd., London. 21 pp.

SACRED AND SECULAR IN ART AND INDUSTRY. A lecture given before the Royal Institution, London, Feb., 1939. John Stephens, Newport, Rhode Island. 31 pp. 1 engraving.

1940 DRAWINGS FROM LIFE. Hague and Gill, Ltd., High Wycombe, Bucks. 36 pp.

THE HUMAN PERSON AND SOCIETY. The Peace Pledge Union, London. (No. 1 of a series of pamphlets under the general title "The Bond of Peace.")

CHRISTIANITY AND THE MACHINE AGE. The Sheldon Press, London. (The Christian News-Letter Books, No. 6.) (Same; The Macmillan Co., N. Y.) 72 pp.

SACRED AND SECULAR. (Six essays.) Illustrated by Tegetmeier. J. M. Dent & Sons, Ltd., London. 199 pp.

AUTOBIOGRAPHY. Jonathan Cape, London. (Also published in New York by The Devin-Adair Company with an Introduction by Beatrice Warde, in 1941, 300 pp. Illustrated.)

1942 LAST ESSAYS. (Nine Essays.) Introduction by Mary Gill. Jonathan Cape, London. 94 pp. Illustrated.

1944 THE STATIONS OF THE CROSS. Some Meditations. The Sower Press, Union Village, N. J. 24 pp.

IT ALL GOES TOGETHER. Selected Essays 1918-1940, Preface by Mary Gill. 23 Essays with illustrations. Introduction by Ananda K. Coomaraswamy. The Devin-Adair Company, New York.

BOOKS IN WHICH ERIC GILL WAS CONTRIBUTING AUTHOR

1906 JOHNSTON, EDWARD: Writing and illuminating and lettering. John Hogg, London. (The Artistic crafts series of technical handbooks.) Chapter XVII: Inscriptions in Stone, by Eric Gill.

1933 MULK-RAJ ANAND: The Hindu view of art; with an introductory essay on art and reality, by Eric Gill. Allen and Unwin, London. 245 pp. Illustrated.

1935 BEEDHAM, R. JOHN: Wood Engraving; with an Introduction and Appendix by Eric Gill. St. Dominic's Press, Ditchling, Sussex. vii, 39 pp. Illustrated.

ILLUSTRATIONS

SWINEHERD

THE MONEY BAG

THE PARDONER'S TALE

A BOOK PLATE

THE SOUL AND THE BRIDEGROOM

INITIAL LETTERS: CUT ON WOOD

INITIAL LETTERS: CUT ON WOOD

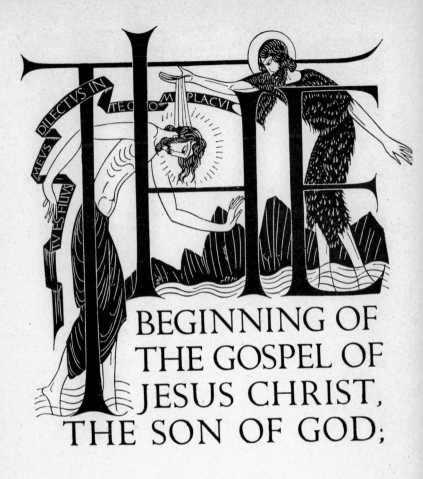

THE BEGINNING OF THE GOSPEL OF JESUS CHRIST, THE SON OF GOD;

CHAPTER OPENING: GOLDEN COCKEREL PRESS EDITION
OF THE FOUR GOSPELS   A

AND

IT CAME TO PASS IN THOSE DAYS, THAT THERE WENT OUT A DECREE

OBLISFUL light, of which the bemes clere
Adorneth al the thridde heuene faire!
O sonnes lief, O Ioues doughter deere,
Pleasaunce of loue, o goodly debonaire,
In gentil hertes ay redy to repaire;
O verray cause of heele and of gladnesse,
I heried be thy myght and thi goodnesse.

In heuene and helle, in erthe and salte see
Is felt thi myght; if that I wel descerne,
As man, brid, best, fisshe, herbe, and grene tree
The fele in tymes with vapour eterne,
GOD loueth, and to loue wol nat werne;
And in this world no lyues creature,
Withouten loue, is worth, or may endure.

Ye Ioues first to thilke effectes glade,
Thorugh which that thynges lyuen alle and be,
Commoeueden, and amorous hym made
On mortal thyng; and as yow list ay ye
Yeue hym in loue ese or aduersite,
And in a thousand formes down hym sente
For loue in erthe, and whom yow liste he hente.

Ye fierse Mars apaisen of his Ire,
And as yow list ye maken hertes digne;
Algates, hem that ye wol sette a fyre,
They dreden shame, and vices they resigne;
Ye don hem curteys ben, fresshe and benigne;
AND heighe or lowe, after a wight entendeth,
The Ioies that he hath youre myght hym sendeth.

BORDER DESIGN AND INITIAL LETTERS FROM CHAUCER'S
"TROILUS AND CRISEYDE": GOLDEN COCKEREL PRESS
EDITION: BODY SET IN CASLON

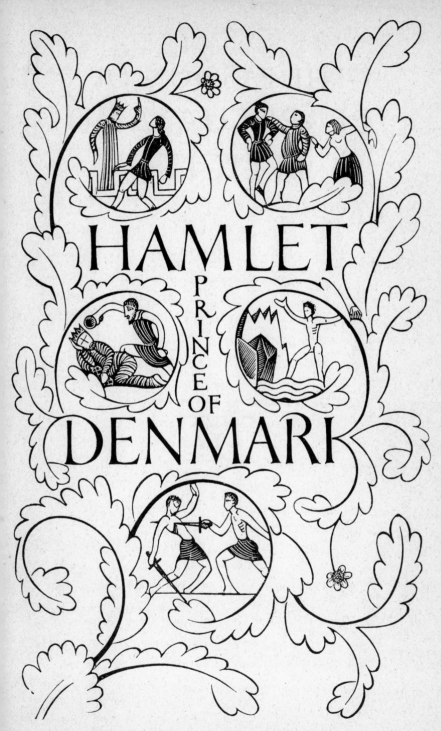

HAMLET

PRINCE OF

DENMARI

THE PASSION OF
PERPETUA AND
FELICITY

MARTYRED AT CARTHAGE A.D. CCIII

A NEW TRANSLATION BY

W. H. SHEWRING

WITH ENGRAVINGS ON WOOD

BY

ERIC GILL

London, 1929

PRINTED FOR 'THE FLEURON'

in Perpetua roman made by the

Lanston Monotype Corporation from the design of

ERIC GILL

TITLE PAGE: THE FIRST USE OF GILL'S PERPETUA TYPE

It shall not hurt me in the name of Jesus Christ. And from beneath the ladder, as though it feared me, it softly put forth its head; and as though I trod on the first step I trod on its head. And I went up, and I saw a very great space of garden, and in the midst a man sitting, white-headed, in

shepherd's clothing, tall, milking his sheep; and standing around in white many thousands. And he raised his head and beheld me and said to me: Welcome, child. And he cried to me, and from the curd he had from the milk he gave me as it were a morsel; and I took it with joined hands and ate it up; and all that stood round said, Amen. And at the sound of their voice I awoke, yet eating I know not what of sweet.

15

A
SPECIMEN OF
THE
PERPETUA ITALIC
Cut by the
Lanston Monotype Corp^n
From the designs of
ERIC GILL

This ken we truly, that as wonder to intellect,
so for the soul desire of beauty is mover and spring;
whence, in whatever his spirit is most moved, a man
wil most be engaged with beauty; and thus in his 'first love'
physical beauty and spiritual are both present
mingled inseparably in his lure: then is he seen
in the ecstasy of earthly passion and of heavenly vision
to fall to idolatry of some specious appearance
as if 'twer very incarnation of his heart's desire,
whether eternal and spiritual, as with Dante it was,
or mere sensuous perfection, or as most commonly
a fusion of both—when if distractedly he hav thought
to mate mortally with an eternal essence
all the delinquencies of his high passion ensue.

PERPETUA ITALIC TYPE

BORDER
DECORATION

an A B C
D E F G H I J K L
abcdefghijklmnopqr
M N O P Q R S T
stuvwxyz 123456789
U V W X Y & Z EG 1932

INCISED ALPHABET ON HOPTON-WOOD STONE

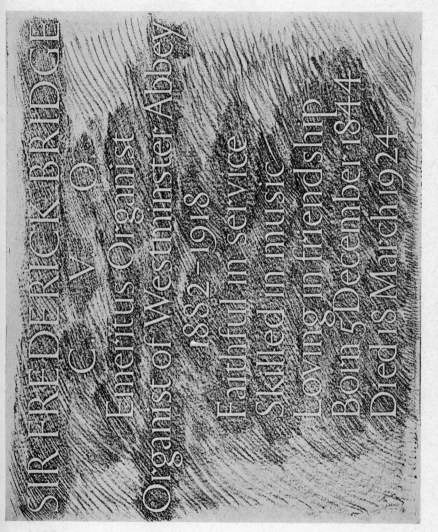

SIR FREDERICK BRIDGE
C.V.O.
Emeritus Organist
Organist of Westminster Abbey
1882–1918
Faithful in service
Skilled in music
Loving in friendship
Born 5 December 1844
Died 18 March 1924

RUBBING OF A CARVED GRAVESTONE INSCRIPTION

DRESS 1920

MADONNA AND CHILD WITH ANGEL

THE CARRYING OF THE CROSS

As the hart de-
sireth the water
brooks; so
Long- eth my
soul after thee,
O God

WOOD ENGRAVING

NAKED GIRL ON GRASS

THE LAST JUDGMENT

SHIP

JESUS FALLS THE THIRD TIME

MOTHER AND CHILD

SPOIL BANK CRUCIFIX

GRAVESTONE WITH ANGEL

CHALICE AND HOST

DESIGN FOR LEAGUE OF NATIONS UNION STAMP

CARVED HEADBOARD OF AN OAK BED